RAG for Text Generation

Practical Techniques to Retrieval-Augmented Generation for Improving Accuracy and Control in Language Models

Martin Dunagan

Copyright © 2024 Martin Dunagan

All rights reserved. No part of this book may be reproduced, stored in a retrieval system, or transmitted, in any form or by any means, electronic, mechanical, photocopying, recording, or otherwise, without the prior written permission of the author, except in the case of brief quotations embodied in critical reviews and certain other noncommercial uses permitted by copyright law.

Table of Contents

Preface..5
Chapter 1: Introduction to Retrieval-Augmented Generation............7
   1.1 Limitations of Language Models..7
   1.2 What is Retrieval-Augmented Generation (RAG)?.....................11
   1.3 Benefits and Advantages..14
   1.4 Types of RAG Architectures..18
   1.5 Key Components of a RAG System.......................................23
Chapter 2: Retrieval Methods for RAG..28
   2.1 Dense Retrieval..28
      2.1.1 Embeddings and Vector Databases................................28
      2.1.2 Approximate Nearest Neighbor Search...........................32
      2.1.3 Efficient Retrieval Techniques.......................................36
   2.2 Sparse Retrieval...40
      2.2.1 TF-IDF and BM25...40
      2.2.2 Inverted Indexes..44
   2.3 Hybrid Retrieval..49
   2.4 Evaluating Retrieval Effectiveness..53
Chapter 3: Generating Text with Retrieved Context.........................58
   3.1 Conditioning Language Models with Retrieved Information.........58
      3.1.1 Fine-tuning for RAG..58
      3.1.2 Prompting with Retrieved Context..................................63
      3.1.3 In-Context Learning with Retrieval.................................67
   3.2 Fusion Techniques for Integrating Retrieved Information...........71
      3.2.1 Concatenation-based Fusion..71
   3.2.2 Attention-based Fusion...75
   3.3 Handling Noise and Irrelevant Retrievals.................................79
Chapter 4: Advanced Techniques in RAG.......................................84
   4.1 Multi-Step Retrieval...84
      4.1.1 Iterative Retrieval and Query Reformulation....................84
   4.2 Contextualized Retrieval..89
   4.3 Personalized Retrieval..93
   4.4 Reinforcement Learning for RAG...97

Chapter 5: Applications of Retrieval-Augmented Generation........102
    5.1 Question Answering...102
    5.2 Dialogue Systems and Conversational AI.............................. 106
    5.3 Text Summarization.. 110
    5.4 Code Generation and Code Completion..................................113
    5.5 Other Applications...117
Chapter 6: Building and Deploying RAG Systems........................122
    6.1 Practical Considerations.. 122
    6.2 Tools, Libraries, and Frameworks for RAG..............................125
    6.3 Data Sources and Preparation... 130
    6.4 Efficiency and Scalability.. 135
    6.5 Ethical Considerations in RAG... 139
Chapter 7: Future Directions of RAG..144
    7.1 Emerging Trends and Research... 144
    7.2 Challenges and Open Problems...147
    7.3 The Future of RAG and Language Models..............................151
Conclusion.. 154

Preface

The rise of large language models (LLMs) has ushered in a new era of natural language processing, enabling machines to generate human-quality text with remarkable fluency. However, these models often struggle with factual accuracy, consistency, and controllability, sometimes generating outputs that are plausible-sounding but ultimately incorrect or nonsensical. This is where Retrieval-Augmented Generation (RAG) comes in.

This book delves into the exciting world of RAG, a powerful technique that enhances language models by grounding their generation in external knowledge sources. By combining the strengths of information retrieval with the generative capabilities of LLMs, RAG offers a promising pathway towards building more reliable, informative, and controllable language technologies.

Whether you are a student, researcher, or practitioner in the field of natural language processing, this book will equip you with the knowledge and tools to understand and implement RAG effectively. We begin with the fundamentals, introducing the core concepts and motivations behind RAG. We then dive deep into various retrieval methods, exploring both dense and sparse approaches, and discuss how to effectively integrate retrieved information into the generation process.

Moving beyond the basics, we explore advanced techniques like multi-step retrieval, contextualized retrieval, and reinforcement learning for RAG, pushing the boundaries of what's possible with this technology. We also showcase the versatility of RAG by examining its applications across diverse domains, including question answering, dialogue systems, text summarization, and code generation.

Throughout the book, we emphasize practical considerations, providing guidance on building and deploying RAG systems in real-world scenarios. We discuss tools, libraries, and frameworks for implementing RAG, offer insights into data source selection and preparation, and address crucial aspects like efficiency, scalability, and ethical considerations.

Finally, we look ahead to the future of RAG, outlining emerging trends, challenges, and opportunities in this rapidly evolving field. We believe that RAG represents a significant step towards building truly intelligent language technologies, and we hope this book will inspire you to explore its potential and contribute to its advancement.

We invite you to embark on this journey into the world of Retrieval-Augmented Generation, where the power of knowledge retrieval meets the creativity of language generation.

Chapter 1: Introduction to Retrieval-Augmented Generation

This chapter sets the stage for our journey, exploring why we need RAG in the first place and how it fundamentally changes the game for language models.

1.1 Limitations of Language Models

Large language models (LLMs) like the one you're interacting with right now are pretty amazing. They Can generate human-quality text, translate languages, write different kinds of creative content, and answer your questions in an informative way. But they're not perfect. Think of them as super-smart parrots – they can mimic human language incredibly well, but they don't truly *understand* the world like we do.

Now, you might have interacted with language models like ChatGPT, and you've probably been blown away by their ability to generate human-like text. They can write stories, poems, articles, and even code![1] But here's the thing: they don't truly understand the world the way we do. They're excellent at mimicking human language, but they lack genuine comprehension.[2]

Let me break down some of the key limitations:

1. Hallucinations: This is a fancy way of saying that language models sometimes make things up.[3] They might present information that sounds perfectly plausible but is factually incorrect or even completely nonsensical.[4] Why does this happen? Well, they learn by analyzing massive amounts of text data, but they don't have a way to cross-check their outputs with reality. It's like they're building a castle in the air – impressive from a distance, but with no real foundation.

For example, you might ask a language model, "Who won the Nobel Prize in Literature in 2023?" Now, let's say this model was trained on data up to 2022. It might confidently give you an answer, but it would be a guess, potentially a very convincing guess, but a guess nonetheless. It doesn't have access to real-time information or the ability to verify its claims.

2. Limited Knowledge: This ties in with the previous point. Language models have a knowledge cut-off point.[5] They are limited by the data they were trained on. Anything that happened after their last training update is essentially a black hole for them. This means they might struggle to answer questions about recent events, provide up-to-date information, or keep up with the latest trends.

Think of it like this: imagine someone went into a coma in 2019 and woke up today. They would have a lot of catching up to do! Similarly, a language model trained before 2019 wouldn't know about the COVID-19 pandemic, the war in Ukraine, or any other major event that has shaped our world since then.

3. Bias and Safety: This is a critical issue. Language models can inherit biases present in their training data.[6] This can lead to outputs that are unfair, discriminatory, or even offensive.[7] For example, if a model is trained on text data that contains gender stereotypes, it might perpetuate those stereotypes in its own generated text.

Moreover, language models can sometimes generate harmful or toxic content, especially if they're not carefully controlled.[8] This is a major concern, as it can have real-world consequences. Imagine a language model being used to generate responses in a customer service chatbot and inadvertently spewing out offensive language – not a good look!

4. Lack of Common Sense and Reasoning: While language models can perform impressive feats of linguistic manipulation, they often

struggle with basic common sense reasoning. They might fail to understand simple cause-and-effect relationships, misinterpret metaphors, or draw illogical conclusions.

For instance, you might tell a language model, "I dropped my phone in the bathtub, and now it's not working." A human would immediately understand that the water damaged the phone. But a language model might come up with a completely unrelated explanation, like "Maybe your battery is dead."

5. Limited Contextual Understanding: Language models often struggle to maintain context over long conversations or complex tasks.[9] They might forget previous interactions, lose track of the main topic, or generate responses that are irrelevant to the current context. This can be frustrating when you're trying to have a meaningful conversation or get a specific task done.

Think of it like trying to have a conversation with someone who has a short-term memory problem. They might repeat themselves, ask the same questions over and over, or suddenly switch topics without warning.

6. Computational Constraints: Training and running large language models requires significant computational resources.[10] This can be a barrier to entry for researchers and developers with limited access to powerful hardware. Even with powerful hardware, generating text from these models can sometimes be slow, which can be a problem for applications that require real-time responses.[11]

7. Difficulty with Ambiguity and Nuance: Human language is full of ambiguities and nuances.[12] We use sarcasm, irony, and humor, and we often express ourselves in ways that require reading between the lines. Language models often struggle with these subtleties, leading to misinterpretations and inappropriate responses.[13]

8. Lack of Emotional Intelligence: Language models don't have emotions or feelings. They can't empathize with users, understand their emotional states, or respond in an emotionally appropriate way. This can be a limitation in applications that require social interaction or emotional support.

These limitations highlight the fact that language models, while powerful, are still a long way from achieving true artificial intelligence.[14] They are tools that can be incredibly useful in certain contexts, but we need to be aware of their limitations and use them responsibly.

Now, don't get me wrong, I'm not trying to paint a gloomy picture here. These limitations are not insurmountable. Researchers are constantly working on new techniques to address these challenges, and we're making progress every day. In fact, one of the most promising approaches is Retrieval-Augmented Generation (RAG), which we'll be exploring in detail throughout this book.[15] But before we get into that, it's crucial to have a solid understanding of the limitations we're trying to overcome.

1.2 What is Retrieval-Augmented Generation (RAG)?

With RAG, we're essentially giving language models a superpower: the ability to tap into external knowledge sources. It's like we're connecting their brains to a vast library of information, allowing them to access and process information far beyond their initial training data.

Think of it this way: instead of relying solely on their internal memory (which, as we discussed, can be limited and outdated), language models can now access a whole world of information on demand. This could be anything – a collection of documents, a knowledge base, the entire internet – you name it!

How does RAG actually work?

Let's break it down step by step:

1. You provide a query or a prompt. This could be a question, a request for information, or a task you want the language model to perform.
2. The RAG system retrieves relevant information from its external knowledge source. This is where the "retrieval" part comes in. The system might use a search engine, a database, or a specialized retrieval model to find documents, passages, or data points that are relevant to your query.
3. The retrieved information is used to "augment" the language model's knowledge. This is where the magic happens. The retrieved information is integrated with the language model, providing it with the context and knowledge it needs to generate a more informed and accurate response.
4. The language model generates a response that is grounded in the retrieved knowledge. This ensures that the response is not only fluent and coherent but also factually accurate and relevant to your query.

Let's look at a concrete example.

Suppose you ask a RAG system, "What are the latest developments in cancer research?"

Here's how the system might respond:

1. Retrieval: The system would first search its knowledge source (e.g., a database of medical research articles) for documents related to cancer research. It might use keywords like "cancer treatment," "clinical trials," "immunotherapy," etc.
2. Augmentation: The system would then select the most relevant documents and feed them to the language model.

This could involve providing the documents as context, extracting key information, or creating a summary.
3. Generation: Finally, the language model would generate a response based on the retrieved information. The response might include summaries of recent clinical trials, breakthroughs in immunotherapy, or new drug developments.

Let's get a bit more technical.

There are different ways to integrate the retrieved information with the language model. Some common techniques include:

- Concatenation: Simply concatenating the retrieved text with the user's query or prompt.
- Attention mechanisms: Using attention mechanisms to allow the language model to focus on the most relevant parts of the retrieved information.
- Fine-tuning: Fine-tuning the language model on a dataset of question-answer pairs, where the answers are derived from the retrieved information.

Here's a simple code example to illustrate how you might concatenate retrieved text with a user's query:

```python
def generate_response(query, retrieved_text):

    """Generates a response using a language model.

    Args:

      query: The user's query.

      retrieved_text: The text retrieved from the knowledge source.
```

```
Returns:

    A string containing the generated response.

"""

# Concatenate the query and retrieved text

input_text = f"Query: {query}\nContext: {retrieved_text}"

# Generate a response using a language model (replace with your actual LLM)

response = language_model.generate(input_text)

return response
```

This is a very basic example, of course. In real-world RAG systems, the integration process is often much more sophisticated, involving complex algorithms and data structures.

Why is RAG so important?

Well, it addresses many of the limitations we discussed earlier. By grounding the language model's output in external knowledge, RAG can:

- Improve accuracy and reduce hallucinations.
- Provide up-to-date information.
- Mitigate biases.
- Enhance control over the generated output.
- Increase transparency and explainability.

RAG makes language models more knowledgeable, reliable, and trustworthy. It opens up a whole new world of possibilities for applications like question answering, dialogue systems, text summarization, and much more.

1.3 Benefits and Advantages

Now we know what Retrieval-Augmented Generation (RAG) is – this cool technique that lets language models access external knowledge. Now, let's talk about why it's such a big deal. What are the real benefits and advantages of using RAG? Why should we care?

Increased Accuracy and Reduced Hallucinations

Remember how we talked about language models sometimes making things up? They can generate text that sounds convincing but is factually incorrect. This is a major problem, especially when we're relying on them for tasks that require accuracy and precision.

RAG helps to address this issue by grounding the language model's output in external knowledge. Instead of relying solely on its internal memory, the model can now access and verify information from reliable sources. This significantly reduces the likelihood of hallucinations and increases the accuracy of the generated text.

Think of it like this: you're writing an article about a historical event. You could rely on your memory and general knowledge, but you're more likely to make mistakes or misinterpret facts. However, if you consult historical documents, books, and research papers, your article will be much more accurate and reliable. RAG does the same thing for language models, providing them with the evidence they need to generate factual and trustworthy content.

Access to Up-to-Date Information

Another limitation of traditional language models is their knowledge cut-off. They are only as good as the data they were trained on. Anything that happened after their last training update is essentially unknown to them.

RAG overcomes this limitation by allowing language models to access the latest information from external sources. This means they can answer questions about recent events, provide up-to-date news, and keep up with the latest trends.

For example, if you ask a traditional language model about the current president of a country, it might give you an outdated answer based on its training data. But a RAG system can access real-time information from the web and provide you with the correct answer.

Reduced Bias and Enhanced Fairness

Language models can inherit biases present in their training data, leading to outputs that are unfair, discriminatory, or even offensive. This is a serious concern, especially in applications where fairness and impartiality are crucial.

RAG can help to mitigate this issue by carefully selecting and curating the external knowledge source. By ensuring that the knowledge source is diverse and representative, we can reduce the risk of bias and promote fairness in the generated output.

For instance, if we're building a RAG system for legal applications, we might use a knowledge source that includes legal documents, case law, and expert opinions from a variety of perspectives. This would help to ensure that the system's outputs are balanced and unbiased.

Enhanced Control and Explainability

One of the challenges with traditional language models is that they can be somewhat of a black box. It's not always clear how they arrive at their answers or why they generate certain outputs. This can make it difficult to control their behavior or understand their reasoning.

RAG provides more control over the generation process by allowing us to specify the knowledge source and influence the retrieval process. This means we can steer the language model towards desired outputs and avoid undesirable ones.

Moreover, RAG can provide insights into the model's decision-making process by revealing the sources it used to generate its response. This makes the system more transparent and explainable, increasing trust and accountability.

Improved Efficiency and Scalability

In some cases, RAG can actually make language models more efficient. By providing the model with relevant information upfront, we can reduce the amount of computation required to generate a response. This can be especially beneficial for tasks that involve large amounts of data or complex reasoning.

Furthermore, RAG can improve the scalability of language models. By decoupling the knowledge retrieval process from the language generation process, we can scale each component independently. This allows us to handle larger datasets and more complex queries without sacrificing performance.

Real-World Examples

RAG is already being used in a variety of real-world applications, including:

- Customer service chatbots: RAG can help chatbots provide more accurate and informative answers to customer queries by accessing knowledge bases and FAQs.
- Search engines: RAG can improve search results by understanding the intent behind user queries and retrieving relevant information from a variety of sources.

- Question answering systems: RAG can power question answering systems that can provide comprehensive and trustworthy answers to complex questions.
- Content creation tools: RAG can assist writers and content creators by providing relevant information, suggesting ideas, and even generating drafts.

These are just a few examples of how RAG is being used to enhance the capabilities of language models and solve real-world problems. As the field continues to evolve, we can expect to see even more innovative applications of this powerful technique.

1.4 Types of RAG Architectures

Let's get a bit more specific and talk about the different ways we can actually build a RAG system. You see, RAG isn't just one thing; there are different architectural approaches, each with its own strengths and weaknesses. It's like choosing the right tool for the job – you need to consider the specific task, the available resources, and the desired outcome.

Dense Retrieval

This approach is all about using embeddings. Now, embeddings are a way to represent words, sentences, or even whole documents as vectors in a high-dimensional space. Think of it like translating text into a numerical format that captures its meaning. The cool thing about embeddings is that similar pieces of text will have similar vectors.

So, in dense retrieval, we use embeddings to represent both the user's query and the documents in our knowledge source. When a user asks a question, we convert it into an embedding and then compare it to the embeddings of all the documents in our database. The documents with the most similar embeddings are considered the most relevant and are retrieved for the language model.

This approach is particularly good at capturing semantic similarity – that is, it can understand that "car" and "automobile" are related even though they are different words. It's also good at handling complex queries with multiple concepts.

However, dense retrieval can be computationally expensive, especially when dealing with very large datasets. Calculating embeddings and comparing them can take time and resources.

Here's a simplified example of how you might implement dense retrieval using Python and a library like Faiss (Facebook AI Similarity Search):

```python
import faiss

# Sample documents and query
documents = [
    "This is a document about dogs.",
    "This is another document about cats.",
    "This is a document about cars."
]

query = "Tell me about pets."

# Generate embeddings (replace with your actual embedding model)
embeddings = embedding_model.encode(documents)

# Create a Faiss index
index = faiss.IndexFlatL2(embeddings.shape[1])
```

```
index.add(embeddings)

# Convert query to embedding

query_embedding = embedding_model.encode([query])[0]

# Search for nearest neighbors

D, I = index.search(np.array([query_embedding]), k=2)   # k=2 to get top 2 results

# Retrieve relevant documents

retrieved_documents = [documents[i] for i in I[0]]

print(retrieved_documents)

# Output: ['This is a document about dogs.',
'This is another document about cats.']
```

In this example, we use an embedding model to generate embeddings for our documents and query. We then create a Faiss index to efficiently search for nearest neighbors. Finally, we retrieve the documents with the most similar embeddings to the query.

Sparse Retrieval

This approach is more traditional and relies on techniques you might have encountered in classic information retrieval systems. It focuses on matching keywords and terms between the query and the documents.

One common technique is TF-IDF (Term Frequency-Inverse Document Frequency). This measures the importance of a word in a document relative to a collection of documents. Words that appear frequently in a document but rarely in the entire collection are considered more important.

Another technique is BM25 (Best Match 25), which is a ranking function that considers the frequency of terms in a document, the length of the document, and the overall frequency of the terms in the collection.

Sparse retrieval often uses inverted indexes to speed up the search process. An inverted index is like a lookup table that maps words to the documents they appear in. This allows the system to quickly find documents that contain specific keywords.

Sparse retrieval is generally faster and more scalable than dense retrieval, especially for very large datasets. However, it might not be as good at capturing semantic similarity or handling complex queries.

Here's a simple example of how you might use TF-IDF in Python with the scikit-learn library:

```python
from sklearn.feature_extraction.text import TfidfVectorizer

# Sample documents and query
documents = [
    "This is a document about dogs.",
    "This is another document about cats.",
    "This is a document about cars."
]

query = "Tell me about pets."
```

```python
# Create a TF-IDF vectorizer
vectorizer = TfidfVectorizer()

# Fit the vectorizer to the documents
vectorizer.fit(documents)

# Transform the documents and query into vectors
document_vectors = vectorizer.transform(documents)

query_vector = vectorizer.transform([query])

# Calculate cosine similarity between query and documents
similarities = cosine_similarity(query_vector, document_vectors).flatten()

# Get the indices of the most similar documents
most_similar_indices = similarities.argsort()[:-3:-1]

# Retrieve relevant documents
retrieved_documents = [documents[i] for i in most_similar_indices]

print(retrieved_documents)

# Output: ['This is a document about dogs.',
'This is another document about cats.']
```

In this example, we use TfidfVectorizer to create a TF-IDF representation of our documents and query. We then calculate the cosine similarity between the query vector and the document vectors to find the most relevant documents.

Hybrid Retrieval

Sometimes, the best approach is to combine both dense and sparse retrieval methods. This is known as hybrid retrieval. By leveraging the strengths of both approaches, we can achieve better overall performance.

For example, we might use dense retrieval to capture semantic similarity and sparse retrieval to handle keyword matching. This can be particularly useful for complex queries that involve both conceptual and specific terms.

Choosing the Right Architecture

So, which architecture is right for you? Well, it depends on your specific needs and resources. Here are some factors to consider:

- Size of the knowledge source: For very large datasets, sparse retrieval might be more efficient.
- Complexity of queries: For complex queries with multiple concepts, dense retrieval might be more effective.
- Computational resources: Dense retrieval can be more computationally expensive than sparse retrieval.
- Desired accuracy: Hybrid retrieval might offer the best balance of accuracy and efficiency.

Ultimately, the best way to choose the right architecture is to experiment and evaluate different approaches on your specific task and dataset.

1.5 Key Components of a RAG System

What are the key components that make up a complete RAG system? It's like understanding the different parts of an engine – each one plays a crucial role in making the whole thing work.

Retrieval Component

This is the workhorse of the RAG system. It's responsible for finding the right information from your knowledge source. Think of it as a librarian who knows exactly where to find the book you're looking for.

The retrieval component can take many forms depending on your needs and the type of knowledge source you're using. Here are a few possibilities:

- Search Engine: For web-based knowledge sources, you might use a search engine like Google or Bing. You can send your query to the search engine's API and get back a list of relevant web pages.
- Database: If your knowledge source is structured data stored in a database, you can use SQL queries to retrieve the relevant information. For example, if you have a database of medical research articles, you might use a query like SELECT * FROM articles WHERE title LIKE '%cancer treatment%' to find articles related to cancer treatment.
- Specialized Retrieval Model: In some cases, you might need a more specialized retrieval model that's tailored to your specific task and knowledge source. This could be a dense retrieval model using embeddings, a sparse retrieval model using TF-IDF, or even a hybrid model combining both approaches.

Knowledge Source

This is the treasure trove of information that your RAG system draws upon. It could be anything – a collection of documents, a knowledge base, a code repository, or even the entire internet!

The choice of knowledge source depends on your application and the type of information you need. Here are a few examples:

- Wikipedia: A great source of general knowledge on a wide range of topics.
- Common Crawl: A massive dataset containing petabytes of web data, including text, images, and metadata.
- Code repositories: Platforms like GitHub and GitLab host millions of open-source code projects, making them valuable resources for code generation tasks.
- Scientific publications: Databases like PubMed and arXiv provide access to a vast collection of scientific articles and research papers.
- Internal documents: Many organizations have their own internal knowledge bases, documentation, and data that can be used as a knowledge source for RAG systems.

Language Model

This is the heart of your RAG system. It's the language model that takes the retrieved information and generates the final output. You have a lot of choices here, from powerful models like GPT-4 to smaller, more specialized models.

The choice of language model depends on your needs and resources. Larger models generally have better performance but require more computational power. Smaller models might be more efficient for specific tasks or resource-constrained environments.

Fusion Component

This component acts as a bridge between the retrieval component and the language model. It takes the retrieved information and prepares it in a way that the language model can understand and use.

There are different ways to do this. Some common techniques include:

- Concatenation: The simplest approach is to simply concatenate the retrieved text with the user's query or prompt. This gives the language model all the information it needs in one go.
- Attention mechanisms: This allows the language model to focus on the most relevant parts of the retrieved information. It's like highlighting the important sentences in a document.
- Summarization: You can use another language model to summarize the retrieved information before feeding it to the main language model. This can be useful when dealing with large amounts of text.

Here's a simplified example of how these components might work together in a RAG system for answering questions about movies:

1. User Query: "Who directed the movie Inception?"
2. Retrieval Component: Sends the query to a knowledge source like Wikipedia and retrieves the page for "Inception."
3. Fusion Component: Extracts the relevant information from the Wikipedia page, such as the director's name (Christopher Nolan).
4. Language Model: Generates a response like "The movie Inception was directed by Christopher Nolan."

This is a very basic example, of course. Real-world RAG systems can be much more complex, involving multiple retrieval steps, sophisticated fusion techniques, and fine-tuned language models.

By understanding the key components of a RAG system and how they interact, you can start to build your own systems and explore the vast potential of this exciting technology. Remember, the key is to choose the right components for your specific needs and combine them in a way that maximizes performance and efficiency.

Chapter 2: Retrieval Methods for RAG

This is where we really start to see how those external knowledge sources we talked about actually get utilized. It's like learning the different ways to navigate a library – you can browse the shelves, use the card catalog, or ask the librarian for help. Each method has its own advantages, and choosing the right one can make all the difference.

2.1 Dense Retrieval

Dense retrieval is a powerful technique that leverages the magic of embeddings. Remember how we talked about representing text as vectors in a high-dimensional space? Well, that's what embeddings are all about. They capture the meaning and relationships between words and sentences in a way that computers can understand.

2.1.1 Embeddings and Vector Databases

Let's break down this "dense retrieval" thing a bit further and talk about embeddings and vector databases. These are the key ingredients that make dense retrieval tick.

Embeddings: Capturing the Essence of Text

You can think of embeddings as a way to translate text into a numerical format that computers can easily understand and work with. But it's not just any numerical format. Embeddings are special because they capture the *meaning* of the text.

Imagine you have three words: "king," "queen," and "prince." In a traditional computer representation, these might just be treated as arbitrary strings of characters. But with embeddings, we can represent them as vectors in a multi-dimensional space, where the position of each vector reflects the meaning of the word.

In this space, the vectors for "king" and "queen" would be closer together because they both represent royalty, while the vector for "prince" might be a bit further away but still closer to "king" than to something completely unrelated like "apple."

This ability to capture semantic relationships is what makes embeddings so powerful for dense retrieval. We can use them to find documents that are similar in meaning to a user's query, even if they don't share the exact same keywords.

How are Embeddings Created?

Embeddings are typically created using machine learning models that are trained on massive amounts of text data. These models learn to represent words and sentences as vectors in a way that captures their semantic relationships.

One popular type of model is called a "word2vec" model. It learns to predict a word based on its surrounding words, and in the process, it learns to represent each word as a vector.

Another popular approach is to use transformer models like BERT or Sentence-BERT. These models are trained on a variety of language tasks, such as language inference and question answering, and they can generate high-quality embeddings that capture the meaning of sentences and paragraphs.

Vector Databases: Storing and Searching Embeddings

Once we have our embeddings, we need a place to store them. That's where vector databases come in. These are specialized databases that are optimized for storing and searching vectors.

Traditional databases are designed to store and retrieve structured data like numbers and text. But vector databases are different.

They are built to handle the unique characteristics of vectors, such as high dimensionality and the need for similarity search.

Think of it like this: if you have a collection of photos, you wouldn't store them in a spreadsheet. You would use a photo album or a photo management software that's designed to handle images. Similarly, vector databases are designed to handle vectors.

Some popular vector databases include:

- Faiss: Developed by Facebook AI Research, Faiss is a highly efficient library for similarity search and clustering of dense vectors. It's known for its speed and scalability, making it a good choice for large-scale applications.
- Pinecone: A fully managed vector database service that makes it easy to deploy and scale dense retrieval applications. It offers a cloud-based solution with features like automatic indexing, query optimization, and data management.
- Milvus: An open-source vector database that supports a variety of indexing and search methods. It's designed to handle massive datasets and complex queries, making it suitable for demanding applications.
- Weaviate: A cloud-native vector database that focuses on semantic search and knowledge graph integration. It allows you to store not only vectors but also relationships between them, enabling more sophisticated search and analysis.

Example: Finding Similar Products

Let's say you're building an e-commerce website and you want to recommend similar products to your customers. You could use embeddings and a vector database to do this.

First, you would generate embeddings for each product description. Then, you would store these embeddings in a vector database. When a customer views a product, you would convert the product description into an embedding and use the vector database to find other products with similar embeddings. These products would then be recommended to the customer.

Code Example: Using Faiss for Similarity Search

Here's a simple example of how you might use Faiss to find similar vectors:

Python

```python
import numpy as np
import faiss
# Generate some random vectors
dimension = 128  # Dimension of the vectors
num_vectors = 10000
vectors = np.random.rand(num_vectors, dimension).astype('float32')
# Create a Faiss index
index = faiss.IndexFlatL2(dimension)  # Using L2 distance
index.add(vectors)
# Create a query vector
query_vector = np.random.rand(1, dimension).astype('float32')
# Search for the nearest neighbors
k = 5  # Number of neighbors to find
D, I = index.search(query_vector, k)
# Print the indices of the nearest neighbors
print(I)
```

In this example, we generate some random vectors and create a Faiss index. We then create a query vector and use the search method to find the k nearest neighbors. The I array contains the indices of the nearest neighbors in the original vectors array.

This is just a basic example, of course. In a real-world application, you would use pre-trained embeddings for your text data and a larger, more diverse dataset. But it gives you a taste of how embeddings and vector databases can be used for similarity search.

2.1.2 Approximate Nearest Neighbor Search

We've discussed embeddings and vector databases. Now, let's tackle a crucial aspect of dense retrieval: finding those "nearest neighbors" efficiently. This is where Approximate Nearest Neighbor (ANN) search comes into play.

You see, when you have a massive collection of embeddings (think millions or even billions of vectors), finding the exact nearest neighbors to a query embedding can be computationally very expensive. It's like trying to find a specific grain of sand on a beach by examining every single grain – it's technically possible, but not very practical.

ANN search offers a clever workaround. It says, "Hey, we don't need to find the *exact* nearest neighbors; we just need to find some vectors that are *pretty close*." By relaxing the requirement for absolute precision, ANN algorithms can significantly speed up the search process, making dense retrieval feasible for large-scale applications.

Think of it like this: if you're looking for a restaurant in a new city, you might not need to find the absolute best restaurant in the entire city. You might be perfectly happy with a restaurant that's highly rated and within a reasonable distance. ANN search operates on a similar principle – it finds good enough solutions quickly.

How Does ANN Search Work?

There are various techniques used in ANN search, each with its own approach to finding those "pretty close" neighbors. Let's explore some of the popular ones:

- Locality-Sensitive Hashing (LSH): This technique uses hash functions to map similar vectors to the same "buckets." Imagine you have a bunch of boxes, and you want to organize your toys. You might put all the cars in one box, all the dolls in another, and so on. LSH does something similar with vectors – it groups similar vectors together, making it easier to find them later.
- Hierarchical Navigable Small World (HNSW): This algorithm creates a graph-like structure that connects the vectors in your database. It's like creating a network of roads between your data points. When you search for a nearest neighbor, you can efficiently navigate through this network to find vectors that are close to your query.
- Product Quantization (PQ): This method compresses the vectors by dividing them into sub-vectors and quantizing each sub-vector. It's like taking a large image and compressing it into a smaller file size. This makes the vectors smaller and faster to search, while still preserving enough information to find approximate nearest neighbors.

Choosing the Right ANN Algorithm

The choice of ANN algorithm depends on various factors, such as:

- Dataset size: Some algorithms are better suited for smaller datasets, while others are designed for massive datasets.

- Dimensionality of vectors: The number of dimensions in your vectors can influence the performance of different algorithms.
- Accuracy requirements: If you need high accuracy, you might choose an algorithm that prioritizes precision over speed.
- Computational resources: Some algorithms require more memory or processing power than others.

Code Example: Using Faiss for ANN Search

Faiss, the library we mentioned earlier, provides implementations of various ANN algorithms. Here's an example of how you might use Faiss to perform ANN search with the IndexIVFFlat index, which uses a quantization technique:

```python
import numpy as np
import faiss

# Generate some random vectors
dimension = 128  # Dimension of the vectors
num_vectors = 100000
vectors = np.random.rand(num_vectors, dimension).astype('float32')

# Create a quantizer
quantizer = faiss.IndexFlatL2(dimension)

# Create an IndexIVFFlat index
index = faiss.IndexIVFFlat(quantizer, dimension, 100)  # 100 is the number of cells
index.train(vectors)
index.add(vectors)
```

```
# Create a query vector
query_vector = np.random.rand(1,
dimension).astype('float32')
# Search for the nearest neighbors
k = 5   # Number of neighbors to find
D, I = index.search(query_vector, k)
# Print the indices of the nearest neighbors
print(I)
```

In this example, we create an **IndexIVFFlat** index, which uses a quantizer to compress the vectors. We then train the index on our dataset and add the vectors. Finally, we perform a search to find the k nearest neighbors.

Real-World Examples

ANN search is used in various applications, including:

- Recommendation systems: Finding similar products or movies based on user preferences.
- Image search: Searching for images that are visually similar to a given image.
- Drug discovery: Identifying molecules that are structurally similar to known drugs.
- Face recognition: Matching faces to identities in a database.

By understanding the principles of ANN search and how it can be implemented with libraries like Faiss, you can unlock the power of dense retrieval for your own RAG applications.

2.1.3 Efficient Retrieval Techniques

Let's talk about some techniques that can make the retrieval process even more efficient. Remember, we're dealing with potentially massive datasets and complex queries, so any optimization we can make can have a big impact on performance.

It's like finding shortcuts and streamlining your workflow – the faster and smoother things run, the better.

Quantization

One way to speed up retrieval is to make the vectors themselves smaller. This is where quantization comes in. It's a technique that reduces the number of bits used to represent each vector. Think of it like compressing a file – you're reducing the size while still preserving the essential information.

There are different quantization methods, but the basic idea is to map the original high-precision vectors to a smaller set of representative vectors. This reduces the storage space required and also speeds up computations, as we're dealing with smaller numbers.

Of course, there's a trade-off here. Quantization introduces some loss of information, which can slightly reduce the accuracy of the nearest neighbor search. But in many cases, this loss is negligible compared to the gains in efficiency.

Indexing: Organizing for Speed

Just like a well-organized library makes it easier to find books, indexing can significantly speed up retrieval in vector databases. An index is a data structure that helps us quickly locate the vectors we're looking for.

There are various indexing techniques, and the best choice depends on the specific characteristics of your data and the type of queries you're running. Some common techniques include:

- Tree-based indexes: These organize the vectors into a tree-like structure, allowing for efficient search by navigating through the branches.

- Hashing-based indexes: These use hash functions to map vectors to buckets, making it faster to find similar vectors.
- Graph-based indexes: These create a graph-like structure that connects the vectors, enabling efficient navigation through the vector space.

Filtering: Narrowing Down the Search

Another way to improve efficiency is to filter out irrelevant vectors before performing the actual nearest neighbor search. This reduces the search space and saves computation time.

For example, if you're searching for documents related to "machine learning," you might filter out documents that don't contain any of the keywords "machine," "learning," or related terms like "AI" or "neural networks." This can significantly reduce the number of vectors you need to compare.

Caching

Caching is a common technique used in many computer systems to speed up access to frequently used data. In the context of dense retrieval, we can cache the embeddings of frequently accessed documents or queries.

This means that when we encounter the same document or query again, we don't need to recompute its embedding. We can simply retrieve it from the cache, saving valuable computation time.

Real-World Example

Let's say you're building a search engine for a large e-commerce website. You have millions of products, each with a detailed description. You want to use dense retrieval to find products that are semantically similar to a user's search query.

To make this efficient, you could use a combination of the techniques we've discussed:

- Quantization: Compress the product embeddings to reduce their size and speed up computations.
- Indexing: Create an index on the vector database to efficiently locate relevant products.
- Filtering: Filter out products that don't contain any of the keywords in the user's query.
- Caching: Cache the embeddings of frequently searched products and queries.

By implementing these techniques, you can ensure that your search engine provides fast and accurate results, even with a massive product catalog.

Code Example: Optimizing Faiss Index

Here's an example of how you might optimize a Faiss index for efficiency:

```python
import numpy as np
import faiss

# Generate some random vectors
dimension = 128   # Dimension of the vectors
num_vectors = 1000000
vectors = np.random.rand(num_vectors, dimension).astype('float32')

# Create a quantizer
quantizer = faiss.IndexFlatL2(dimension)

# Create an IndexIVFFlat index with quantization
index = faiss.IndexIVFFlat(quantizer, dimension, 100)   # 100 is the number of cells

index.train(vectors)
```

```
index.add(vectors)
# Add some optimizations
index.nprobe = 10  # Number of cells to explore during search
faiss.omp_set_num_threads(4)  # Use multiple threads for parallel processing
# Create a query vector
query_vector = np.random.rand(1, dimension).astype('float32')
# Search for the nearest neighbors
k = 5  # Number of neighbors to find
D, I = index.search(query_vector, k)
# Print the indices of the nearest neighbors
print(I)
```

In this example, we use the nprobe parameter to control the number of cells explored during the search. We also use faiss.omp_set_num_threads to enable parallel processing, which can significantly speed up the search on multi-core machines.

These are just a few examples of the many optimization techniques available in Faiss. By exploring the documentation and experimenting with different parameters, you can fine-tune your Faiss index for maximum efficiency.

2.2 Sparse Retrieval

Sparse retrieval takes a different approach. It focuses on matching keywords and terms between the query and the documents. This is often done using traditional information retrieval techniques like TF-IDF and BM25.

2.2.1 TF-IDF and BM25

Let's explore the world of sparse retrieval. This approach takes a different tack than dense retrieval, focusing on the specific words and terms that appear in your documents and queries. It's like searching for a book in a library by looking at the words in the title or the index – you're looking for specific matches rather than overall similarity.

Two of the most popular techniques in sparse retrieval are TF-IDF and BM25. These are like the dynamic duo of keyword-based search, helping us find the documents that are most relevant to a user's query.

TF-IDF

TF-IDF stands for Term Frequency-Inverse Document Frequency. It's a mouthful, but the concept is actually quite simple. It's a way to measure how important a word is to a document in a collection of documents.

Let's break it down:

- Term Frequency (TF): This measures how often a word appears in a document. The more often a word appears, the more important it is likely to be to that document. For example, in a document about dogs, the word "dog" will likely appear many times, indicating its importance.
- Inverse Document Frequency (IDF): This measures how rare a word is across the entire collection of documents. The rarer a word is, the more discriminating it is. For example, the word "the" appears in almost every document, so it's not very helpful in distinguishing between documents. But a word like "algorithm" is more specific and therefore more useful for identifying relevant documents.

By combining TF and IDF, we get a score that reflects the importance of a word to a document relative to the entire collection. This score can then be used to rank documents based on their relevance to a query.

Example: Searching for News Articles

Let's say you're searching for news articles about the latest developments in artificial intelligence. You might use a search engine that uses TF-IDF to rank the articles.

Articles that frequently mention terms like "artificial intelligence," "machine learning," and "deep learning" would likely have higher TF-IDF scores and would be ranked higher in the search results. Articles that only mention these terms once or twice, or that focus on other topics, would have lower scores and would be ranked lower.

BM25

BM25 (Best Match 25) is a ranking function that builds upon TF-IDF. It's like TF-IDF's more sophisticated cousin. It takes into account additional factors that can affect the relevance of a document, such as:

- Document length: Longer documents tend to have more words, which can inflate their TF-IDF scores. BM25 adjusts for this by normalizing the scores based on document length.
- Average document length: BM25 also considers the average length of documents in the collection. This helps to ensure that the scores are comparable across different collections.

BM25 is often considered to be more effective than TF-IDF, especially for longer documents and larger collections. It's widely used in modern search engines and information retrieval systems.

Code Example: Using Scikit-learn for TF-IDF

Here's an example of how you might use the scikit-learn library in Python to calculate TF-IDF scores:

Python

```python
from sklearn.feature_extraction.text import TfidfVectorizer

# Sample documents
documents = [
    "This is a document about dogs.",
    "This is another document about cats.",
    "This is a document about cars and dogs."
]

# Create a TF-IDF vectorizer
vectorizer = TfidfVectorizer()

# Fit the vectorizer to the documents
vectorizer.fit(documents)

# Transform the documents into a matrix of TF-IDF features
tfidf_matrix = vectorizer.transform(documents)

# Print the TF-IDF matrix
print(tfidf_matrix.toarray())
```

This code will output a matrix where each row represents a document and each column represents a word in the vocabulary. The values in the matrix represent the[1] TF-IDF scores for each word in each document.

You can then use this matrix to perform various tasks, such as:

- Finding similar documents: Calculate the cosine similarity between the TF-IDF vectors of different documents.
- Ranking documents for a query: Calculate the TF-IDF score for a query and compare it to the scores of the documents.
- Identifying important words in a document: Look for the words with the highest TF-IDF scores in a document.

Real-World Applications

TF-IDF and BM25 are used in a wide range of applications, including:

- Search engines: Ranking web pages and other documents based on their relevance to a user's search query.
- Information retrieval systems: Finding relevant documents in large collections, such as libraries, archives, and databases.
- Text mining: Extracting key information and insights from text data.
- Recommendation systems: Recommending items to users based on their interests and preferences.

By understanding the principles of TF-IDF and BM25, you can gain a deeper understanding of how sparse retrieval works and how it can be used to power various applications.

2.2.2 Inverted Indexes

This is one of those behind-the-scenes heroes that you might not see directly, but it plays a vital role in making search efficient and fast.

Think of it like this: you have a massive library with millions of books. If you want to find all the books that mention "artificial intelligence," you could go through each book page by page, scanning for that phrase. But that would take forever!

An inverted index offers a much smarter approach. It's like having a card catalog for your library, but instead of listing books by title or author, it lists them by the words they contain. So, you could simply look up "artificial intelligence" in the index, and it would immediately tell you which books contain that phrase.

How Does an Inverted Index Work?

An inverted index is essentially a mapping between words and the documents they appear in. It consists of two main components:

1. Vocabulary: A list of all the unique words (or terms) that appear in your collection of documents.
2. Postings lists: For each word in the vocabulary, a list of the documents that contain that word.

Let's illustrate this with a simple example. Suppose you have three documents:

- **Document 1:** "The dog chased the cat."
- **Document 2:** "The cat sat on the mat."
- **Document 3:** "The dog ate the bone."

The vocabulary for this collection would be:

```
["the", "dog", "chased", "cat", "sat", "on", "mat", "ate", "bone"]
```

And the inverted index would look like this:

```
"the": [1, 2, 3]

"dog": [1, 3]
```

```
"chased": [1]

"cat": [1, 2]

"sat": [2]

"on": [2]

"mat": [2]

"ate": [3]

"bone": [3]
```

As you can see, each word is associated with a list of document IDs. So, if you want to find all documents containing the word "cat," you simply look up "cat" in the index and get the list [1, 2].

Inverted indexes are incredibly efficient for keyword-based search because they allow us to quickly locate the documents that contain specific words. Instead of scanning through every document, we can simply look up the words in the index and retrieve the corresponding postings lists.

This is especially beneficial when dealing with large collections of documents and complex queries. For example, if you want to find all documents that contain the words "artificial intelligence" AND "machine learning," you can simply retrieve the postings lists for both terms and find the documents that appear in both lists.

Real-World Examples

Inverted indexes are used in a wide variety of applications, including:

- Search engines: They are the backbone of most web search engines, allowing them to quickly find relevant web pages for a given query.

- Email search: They are used to index emails so you can quickly search for messages containing specific keywords or phrases.
- Full-text search in databases: They enable efficient search within text fields in databases.
- Document retrieval systems: They are used to index large collections of documents, such as legal documents, scientific articles, and news archives.

Code Example: Building an Inverted Index in Python

Here's a simple example of how you might build an inverted index in Python:

Python

```
from collections import defaultdict

def build_inverted_index(documents):
  """Builds an inverted index from a list of documents.

  Args:
    documents: A list of documents, where each document is a string.

  Returns:
    A dictionary representing the inverted index, where keys are words and
    values are lists of document IDs.
  """
  inverted_index = defaultdict(list)
```

```python
    for doc_id, document in enumerate(documents):
        words = document.lower().split()
        for word in words:
            inverted_index[word].append(doc_id)
    return inverted_index

# Sample documents
documents = [
    "The dog chased the cat.",
    "The cat sat on the mat.",
    "The dog ate the bone."
]

# Build the inverted index
index = build_inverted_index(documents)

# Print the inverted index
for word, doc_ids in index.items():
    print(f'"{word}": {doc_ids}')
```

This code defines a function build_inverted_index that takes a list of documents and returns a dictionary representing the inverted index. It iterates through the documents, splits them into words, and adds each word to the index along with the corresponding document ID.

This is a basic example, of course. In a real-world application, you would likely use more sophisticated techniques for tokenization, stemming, and stop word removal to improve the quality of the index.

By understanding how inverted indexes work and how to implement them, you can gain a deeper appreciation for the power of sparse retrieval and its ability to efficiently handle large-scale text data.

2.3 Hybrid Retrieval

We've discussed dense retrieval with its fancy embeddings and sparse retrieval with its keyword-matching prowess. Now, what if I told you we could combine the best of both worlds? That's exactly what hybrid retrieval is all about! It's like having a toolbox with both a hammer and a screwdriver – you can choose the right tool for the job or even use them together for those extra tricky tasks.

Dense and sparse retrieval each have their own strengths and weaknesses. Dense retrieval excels at capturing semantic similarity, understanding the meaning behind words, and handling complex queries with multiple concepts. But it can be computationally expensive, especially for massive datasets.

Sparse retrieval, on the other hand, is generally faster and more scalable, especially for keyword-based search. But it might miss out on those subtle semantic connections and struggle with queries that require a deeper understanding of the text.

So, by combining these two approaches, we can create a more robust and versatile retrieval system. It's like having a superhero team where each member brings their unique skills to the table.

How Does Hybrid Retrieval Work?

There are different ways to combine dense and sparse retrieval. Here are a few common strategies:

- Sequential combination: This involves using one retrieval method as a first step to narrow down the search space, and then using the other method to refine the results. For example, you might use sparse retrieval to quickly identify documents that contain relevant keywords, and then use dense retrieval to rank those documents based on their semantic similarity to the query.
- Parallel combination: This involves running both retrieval methods simultaneously and then combining the results. You might use different weighting schemes to give more importance to one method or the other, depending on the specific query and context.
- Feature combination: This involves combining the features used by both methods. For example, you might combine the TF-IDF scores from sparse retrieval with the embedding vectors from dense retrieval to create a new representation that captures both keyword and semantic information.

Real-World Examples

Hybrid retrieval is gaining popularity in various applications, including:

- E-commerce search: Combining keyword matching with semantic similarity can help users find products that are both relevant to their search terms and match their overall intent. For example, a search for "red dress" could return dresses that are not only red but also similar in style to other dresses the user has previously viewed or purchased.
- Question answering: Hybrid retrieval can help find the most relevant passages from a large corpus of text to answer a user's question. Sparse retrieval can quickly identify passages containing relevant keywords, while dense retrieval can ensure that the selected passages truly answer the question semantically.

- Recommender systems: Combining collaborative filtering (based on user behavior) with content-based filtering (based on item features) can lead to more accurate and personalized recommendations.

Code Example: Combining TF-IDF and Embeddings

Here's a simplified example of how you might combine TF-IDF and embeddings in Python:

```python
from sklearn.feature_extraction.text import TfidfVectorizer

from sklearn.metrics.pairwise import cosine_similarity

# Sample documents[1] and query

documents = [

    "This is a document about dogs.",

    "This is another document about cats.",

    "This is a document about cars and dogs."

]

query = "Tell me about pets."

# Calculate TF-IDF scores

vectorizer = TfidfVectorizer()

tfidf_matrix = vectorizer.fit_transform(documents)
```

```
query_tfidf = vectorizer.transform([query])

# Calculate embedding similarities (replace with
your actual embedding model)

embeddings = embedding_model.encode(documents)

query_embedding =
embedding_model.encode([query])[0]

embedding_similarities =
cosine_similarity([query_embedding],
embeddings).flatten()

# Combine TF-IDF and embedding scores (simple
averaging)

combined_scores = (tfidf_matrix *
query_tfidf.T).toarray().flatten() +
embedding_similarities

combined_scores /= 2

# Get the indices of the most similar documents

most_similar_indices =
combined_scores.argsort()[:-3:-1]

# Retrieve relevant documents

retrieved_documents = [documents[i] for i in
most_similar_indices]

print(retrieved_documents)
```

In this example, we first calculate the TF-IDF scores and embedding similarities separately. Then, we combine these scores using a simple averaging method. You could experiment with different weighting schemes to fine-tune the combination. Finally, we retrieve the documents with the highest combined scores.

This is a basic illustration, and in a real-world scenario, you would likely use more sophisticated techniques for combining the scores and fine-tuning the retrieval process. By understanding the principles of hybrid retrieval and experimenting with different combination strategies, you can create more powerful and versatile retrieval systems that leverage the strengths of both dense and sparse methods. This can lead to significant improvements in accuracy, efficiency, and overall performance in various RAG applications.

2.4 Evaluating Retrieval Effectiveness

Okay, we've covered a lot of ground exploring different retrieval methods, from dense and sparse to hybrid approaches. But how do we know if our retrieval system is actually doing a good job? How do we measure its effectiveness? That's where evaluation comes in. It's like taking a test after studying – it helps you assess your understanding and identify areas for improvement.

In the context of retrieval, evaluation means measuring how well our system can find the truly relevant information from our knowledge source. We want to make sure that it's not just retrieving random documents but actually finding the ones that are most useful for answering a user's query or completing a task.

Metrics for Measuring Retrieval Effectiveness

There are several metrics we can use to evaluate retrieval effectiveness. Let's explore some of the most common ones:

- Recall: This metric tells us how many of the truly relevant documents our system is able to retrieve. It's like a fishing net – a high recall means you're catching most of the fish in the lake. More formally, it's the number of relevant

documents retrieved divided by the total number of relevant documents in the collection.
- Precision:[1] This metric tells us how many of the retrieved documents are actually relevant. It's like aiming for a target – a high precision means you're hitting the bullseye most of the time. Formally, it's the number of relevant documents retrieved divided by the total number of documents retrieved.
- F1-score: This metric combines recall and precision into a single score. It's like getting a combined score for both your fishing skills and your aiming skills. The F1-score is the harmonic mean of precision and recall, which means it gives more weight to the lower of the two scores. This is useful because it encourages a balance between recall and precision.
- Mean Average Precision (MAP): This metric takes into account the ranking of the retrieved documents. It's like judging a singing competition – you not only want to select the good singers but also rank them in the right order. MAP calculates the average precision at each position in the ranked list of retrieved documents and then averages these precision values over all queries.
- Normalized Discounted Cumulative Gain (NDCG): This metric is similar to MAP but gives more weight to documents that are ranked higher in the list. It's like giving more points to the singers who perform better earlier in the competition. NDCG measures the gain of each document based on its relevance and position in the ranking and then normalizes it to a scale from 0 to 1.

The choice of metric depends on your specific needs and the nature of your application. If you need to find all the relevant documents, even if it means retrieving some irrelevant ones, then recall is important. If you need to be very sure that the retrieved documents are relevant, then precision is crucial. And if you need a balance between the two, then F1-score or MAP might be good choices.

Real-World Example: Evaluating a Search Engine

Let's say you're evaluating the performance of a search engine. You could use a dataset of queries and their corresponding relevant documents. You would then run the queries through the search engine and measure the retrieval effectiveness using one or more of the metrics we've discussed.

For example, you might calculate the MAP for a set of queries to see how well the search engine ranks the relevant documents. Or you might calculate the recall to see how many of the relevant documents the search engine is able to find.

Code Example: Calculating Recall and Precision in Python

Here's a simple example of how you might calculate recall and precision in Python:

```python
def calculate_recall_precision(retrieved_documents, relevant_documents):

    """Calculates recall and precision for a set of retrieved documents.

    Args:

        retrieved_documents: A list of document IDs retrieved by the system.

        relevant_documents: A list of document IDs that are truly relevant.
```

    Returns:

        A tuple containing the recall and precision values.

    """

    num_relevant_retrieved = len(set(retrieved_documents) & set(relevant_documents))

    recall = num_relevant_retrieved / len(relevant_documents)

    precision = num_relevant_retrieved / len(retrieved_documents)

    return recall, precision

Example usage

retrieved_docs = [1, 2, 5, 7, 10]

relevant_docs = [1, 2, 6, 8, 10]

recall, precision = calculate_recall_precision(retrieved_docs, relevant_docs)

print(f"Recall: {recall:.2f}")

print(f"Precision: {precision:.2f}")

This code defines a function calculate_recall_precision that takes two lists of document IDs – the retrieved documents and the truly relevant documents – and calculates the recall and precision.

While these metrics provide valuable quantitative measures of retrieval effectiveness, it's important to remember that they don't tell the whole story. Qualitative evaluation is also important. This involves looking at the actual retrieved documents and assessing their relevance and usefulness in the context of the user's query or task.

For example, you might examine the top-ranked documents to see if they are truly the most relevant and informative. You might also look for patterns in the retrieved documents to identify any biases or limitations in the retrieval system.

By combining quantitative and qualitative evaluation, you can gain a comprehensive understanding of your retrieval system's performance and identify areas for improvement. This will help you build more effective and reliable RAG systems that can truly meet the needs of your users.

Chapter 3: Generating Text with Retrieved Context

We've spent a good amount of time talking about how to find the right information using various retrieval methods. Now, let's get to the exciting part – actually using that information to generate text! It's like having all the ingredients for a delicious meal and finally getting to cook. This is where the "generation" in Retrieval-Augmented Generation (RAG) truly shines.

3.1 Conditioning Language Models with Retrieved Information

Remember those powerful language models we talked about? They're great at generating human-like text, but they need the right input to produce relevant and accurate outputs. That's where the retrieved context comes in. It's like giving the language model a cheat sheet or a set of notes to guide its writing.

There are different ways to "condition" a language model with retrieved information. Let's explore some of the most common techniques:

3.1.1 Fine-tuning for RAG

These large language models are like talented but somewhat generic students. They have a broad understanding of language and can generate impressive text, but they might not be experts in any particular subject.

Fine-tuning is like giving these students specialized training in a specific domain. We take a pre-trained language model and further train it on a dataset that's relevant to our RAG application. This helps the model adapt to the specific characteristics of our knowledge source and learn to generate more accurate and relevant responses.

Think of it like this: you have a friend who's a great writer, but they've never written a news article before. You could give them some tips and guidelines, but they might still struggle to capture the style and tone of a news article. However, if you give them a bunch of news articles to read and analyze, they'll start to get a feel for it and their writing will improve.

That's essentially what fine-tuning does for language models. We expose them to a dataset of examples that are relevant to our task, and they learn to adapt their behavior accordingly.

How Does Fine-tuning Work in RAG?

In the context of RAG, we typically fine-tune the language model on a dataset of question-answer pairs, where the answers are derived from our retrieved information. This means we need to create a dataset where each example consists of:

1. A question: This could be a user query or any question that we want the model to be able to answer.
2. Relevant context: This is the information retrieved from our knowledge source that's relevant to the question.
3. An answer: This is the correct answer to the question, based on the retrieved context.

For example, if we're building a RAG system for answering questions about movies, our dataset might look like this:

Question	Relevant Context	Answer
Who directed the movie Inception?	Inception is a 2010 science fiction action film	Christopher Nolan

What is the plot of the movie The Matrix?	The Matrix is a 1999 science fiction action film written and directed by the Wachowskis. It depicts a dystopian future in which reality as perceived by most humans[1] is actually a simulated reality called "the Matrix", created by sentient machines.[2]	written and directed by Christopher Nolan.	The Matrix depicts a dystopian future where reality is a simulation created by machines.
..	..		..

We can then use this dataset to fine-tune our language model. During fine-tuning, the model learns to generate answers that are consistent with the information in the retrieved context.

Benefits of Fine-tuning for RAG

Fine-tuning offers several benefits for RAG:

- Improved accuracy: By fine-tuning on a relevant dataset, we can improve the accuracy of the generated answers. The model learns to better understand the nuances of the domain and generate responses that are more faithful to the retrieved information.
- Better relevance: Fine-tuning helps the model generate answers that are more relevant to the user's query. It learns

to focus on the important information in the retrieved context and avoid generating irrelevant or tangential responses.
- Enhanced consistency: Fine-tuning can help ensure that the generated answers are consistent with the information in our knowledge source. This is important for maintaining the integrity and reliability of our RAG system.
- Adaptation to specific domains: Fine-tuning allows us to adapt the language model to specific domains or knowledge sources. This can be particularly useful when dealing with specialized or niche areas of knowledge.

Code Example: Fine-tuning with Hugging Face Transformers

Here's a simplified example of how you might fine-tune a language model using the Hugging Face Transformers library in Python:

```python
from transformers import AutoModelForQuestionAnswering, TrainingArguments, Trainer

# Load the pre-trained model

model_name = "bert-base-uncased"

model = AutoModelForQuestionAnswering.from_pretrained(model_name)

# Define the training arguments

training_args = TrainingArguments(
    output_dir="./results",
```

```
    num_train_epochs=3,
    per_device_train_batch_size=8,³
    learning_rate=5e-5,
)
# Create a Trainer instance
trainer = Trainer(
    model=model,
    args=training_args,
    train_dataset=train_dataset,  # Your training dataset
)
# Fine-tune the model
trainer.train()
# Save the fine-tuned model
model.save_pretrained("./fine_tuned_model")
```

In this example, we load a pre-trained question-answering model from the Hugging Face Model Hub. We then define the training arguments, such as the number of epochs, batch size, and learning rate. We create a Trainer instance and use it to fine-tune the model on our training dataset. Finally, we save the fine-tuned model for later use.

Real-World Applications

Fine-tuning is used in various RAG applications, including:

- Customer service chatbots: Fine-tuning can help chatbots provide more accurate and relevant answers to customer queries based on the company's knowledge base.
- Technical support systems: Fine-tuning can help support agents quickly find solutions to technical problems by providing them with relevant information from technical documentation.
- Educational platforms: Fine-tuning can help create personalized learning experiences by tailoring the content and difficulty level to individual students.

By understanding the principles of fine-tuning and leveraging the tools available in libraries like Hugging Face Transformers, you can significantly enhance the performance and effectiveness of your RAG systems.

3.1.2 Prompting with Retrieved Context

Language models are like eager assistants waiting for instructions. They have a lot of knowledge and skills, but they need to be told what to do. That's where prompting comes in. It's like giving the model a clear and concise set of instructions to guide its generation.

Think of it like this: you have a friend who's a talented artist, but they need some inspiration to get started. You could give them a specific theme or a set of colors to work with, and they'll create something amazing based on those prompts.

Similarly, prompting in RAG involves providing the language model with a specific context or a set of guidelines to steer its generation process. We use the information retrieved from our knowledge source to create a prompt that guides the model towards generating a relevant and accurate response.

How Does Prompting Work in RAG?

In RAG, we typically include the retrieved information as part of the prompt. This gives the language model the necessary background knowledge and context to understand the user's query and generate an appropriate response.

Here are a few ways to incorporate retrieved context into a prompt:

- Direct inclusion: We can simply include the retrieved text directly in the prompt. This is the most straightforward approach and can be effective for short pieces of information.
- Summarization: If the retrieved information is lengthy, we can summarize it before including it in the prompt. This helps to keep the prompt concise and focused.
- Question-answer format: We can structure the prompt as a question-answer pair, where the question is the user's query and the answer is the retrieved information. This can help the model understand the relationship between the query and the context.
- Instruction-based prompts: We can provide specific instructions to the model on how to use the retrieved information. For example, we might instruct the model to "summarize the following text" or "answer the following question based on the provided context."

Benefits of Prompting in RAG

Prompting offers several benefits for RAG:

- Flexibility: Prompting is a very flexible technique. We can tailor the prompt to the specific query and context, providing the language model with the exact information it needs to generate a relevant response.

- **Control:** Prompting gives us more control over the generation process. We can guide the model towards specific outputs by providing clear and concise instructions.
- **Efficiency:** Prompting can be very efficient, especially for simple queries or when the retrieved information is concise. We don't need to fine-tune the model or perform complex fusion operations.
- **Transparency:** Prompting makes the generation process more transparent. We can clearly see how the retrieved information is being used to guide the model's response.

Code Example: Prompting with Python

Here's a simple example of how you might use prompting in Python:

```python
def generate_response(query, retrieved_context):
    """Generates a response using a language model and a prompt.

    Args:
        query: The user's query.
        retrieved_context: The context retrieved from the knowledge source.

    Returns:
        A string containing the generated response.
    """

    # Create a prompt with the retrieved context
```

```
    prompt = f"Context:
{retrieved_context}\nQuestion: {query}"

    # Generate a response using a language model
(replace with your actual LLM)

    response = language_model.generate(prompt)

    return response
```

In this example, we create a prompt by concatenating the retrieved context with the user's query. We then use a language model to generate a response based on this prompt.

Real-World Examples

Prompting is used in various RAG applications, including:

- Search engines: Search engines can use prompts to generate more informative and relevant snippets for search results.
- Question answering systems: Question answering systems can use prompts to guide the language model towards generating accurate and concise answers.
- Dialogue systems: Dialogue systems can use prompts to maintain context and generate coherent responses in multi-turn conversations.
- Code generation: Code generation tools can use prompts to generate code snippets based on natural language descriptions.

By understanding the principles of prompting and experimenting with different prompt engineering techniques, you can significantly enhance the control, flexibility, and effectiveness of your RAG systems.

3.1.3 In-Context Learning with Retrieval

In-context learning is a relatively new and exciting area of research in natural language processing. It's still being actively explored, but it has the potential to revolutionize how we interact with and utilize language models.

How Does In-Context Learning Work in RAG?

In the context of RAG, we can use retrieved information as examples for in-context learning. Instead of explicitly training the language model on a specific task or dataset, we provide it with a few examples of questions and answers, and the model can then generalize from those examples to answer new questions.

Think of it like this: you're trying to teach a child how to identify different types of animals. You could show them pictures of a cat, a dog, and a bird, and tell them the names of each animal. Then, when you show them a picture of a horse, they might be able to correctly identify it as a horse, even though they've never seen a horse before.

Similarly, in RAG, we can retrieve examples of questions and answers from our knowledge source and provide them to the language model as context. The model can then use these examples to learn the underlying patterns and relationships and generate answers to new questions.

For example, if a user asks, "What are the side effects of aspirin?", we could retrieve a few examples of questions and answers about the side effects of other medications:

Example 1: Question: What are the side effects of ibuprofen? Answer: Common side effects of ibuprofen include stomach upset, nausea, and headache.

Example 2: Question: What are the side effects of acetaminophen? Answer: Acetaminophen can cause liver damage if taken in large doses.

Question: What are the side effects of aspirin?

By providing these examples, we can guide the language model to generate an answer about the side effects of aspirin, even though it hasn't been explicitly trained on that specific question.

Benefits of In-Context Learning for RAG

In-context learning offers several advantages for RAG:

- Data efficiency: In-context learning can be very data-efficient. We don't need to create large labeled datasets for fine-tuning. A few well-chosen examples can be enough to guide the model's behavior.
- Adaptability: In-context learning allows the model to adapt to new tasks and domains quickly. We can simply provide new examples, and the model can learn to generate relevant responses without any further training.
- Flexibility: In-context learning is very flexible. We can use it for a wide range of tasks, from question answering to text summarization to code generation.
- Reduced training costs: In-context learning can reduce the computational costs associated with training and fine-tuning large language models.

Challenges and Considerations

While in-context learning is a promising technique, there are also some challenges and considerations:

- Example selection: The quality and relevance of the examples are crucial for effective in-context learning. We

need to carefully select examples that are representative of the task and domain.
- Prompt engineering: The way we present the examples and the question to the model can significantly impact its performance. We need to carefully craft the prompt to guide the model's attention and reasoning.
- Model limitations: In-context learning is still a relatively new area of research, and there are limitations to what current language models can achieve. The model's ability to generalize from examples can vary depending on the complexity of the task and the quality of the examples.

Real-World Examples

In-context learning is being explored in various RAG applications, including:

- Personalized assistants: In-context learning can help personalize assistants learn user preferences and provide more tailored responses.
- Code generation: In-context learning can help code generation tools generate code snippets based on a few examples of similar code.
- Chatbots: In-context learning can help chatbots adapt to new conversation topics and provide more relevant responses.

Code Example: In-Context Learning with Python

Here's a simplified example of how you might use in-context learning in Python:

```python
def generate_response(query, examples):
```

```
    """Generates a response using a language model
and in-context learning.

    Args:

        query: The user's query.

        examples: A list of examples in the format
"Question: ... Answer: ..."

    Returns:

        A string containing the generated response.
    """

    # Create a prompt with the examples and the query
    prompt = "\n".join(examples) + f"\nQuestion: {query}"

    # Generate a response using a language model (replace with your actual LLM)
    response = language_model.generate(prompt)

    return response
```

In this example, we create a prompt by concatenating the examples with the user's query. We then use a language model to generate a response based on this prompt.

By understanding the principles of in-context learning and experimenting with different example selection and prompt engineering techniques, you can leverage the power of this approach to create more adaptable and efficient RAG systems.

3.2 Fusion Techniques for Integrating Retrieved Information

Once we have the retrieved information, we need to integrate it with the language model's input. This is where fusion techniques come in. They're like chefs who combine different ingredients to create a delicious dish.

3.2.1 Concatenation-based Fusion

Alright, let's get down to the nitty-gritty of how we actually combine the retrieved information with the language model's input. This is where fusion techniques come into play. They're like the bridge that connects the retrieved knowledge to the language model's generation process.

One of the simplest and most straightforward fusion techniques is concatenation. It's like taking two pieces of a puzzle and simply fitting them together. We take the retrieved text and the user's query (or prompt) and combine them into a single input sequence.

Think of it like this: you have a recipe for a cake, and you also have a list of ingredients. Concatenation would be like writing the recipe first and then listing the ingredients below it, creating a single document with all the information.

How Does Concatenation Work in RAG?

In RAG, concatenation typically involves the following steps:

1. Retrieve relevant information: We use our retrieval component to find the most relevant documents or passages from our knowledge source based on the user's query.
2. Format the retrieved information: We might need to format the retrieved information to make it suitable for concatenation. This could involve removing irrelevant parts, adding separators, or converting it to a specific format.

3. Concatenate the information: We combine the formatted retrieved information with the user's query or prompt. This creates a single input sequence that will be fed to the language model.
4. Generate the response: We use the language model to generate a response based on the concatenated input sequence.

Example:

Let's say a user asks, "What is the capital of France?" We retrieve the following sentence from Wikipedia: "Paris is the capital and most populous city of France."

We can then concatenate this sentence with the user's query:

```
Input: "What is the capital of France? Paris is
the capital and most populous city of France."
```

This combined input is then fed to the language model, which can easily extract the answer "Paris."

Benefits of Concatenation

Concatenation offers several advantages:

- Simplicity: It's very simple to implement and understand. We don't need any complex algorithms or data structures.
- Efficiency: It's computationally efficient, as it doesn't require any significant processing or transformation of the retrieved information.
- Preservation of information: It preserves the original retrieved information without any modification, which can be important for certain applications.

Limitations of Concatenation

However, concatenation also has some limitations:

- Length limitations: Language models have a limited input length. If the retrieved information is too long, we might not be able to concatenate it with the query without exceeding the model's input limit.
- Lack of focus: Concatenation treats all the retrieved information equally. The language model doesn't have any guidance on which parts of the information are most relevant to the query.
- Potential for noise: If the retrieved information contains irrelevant or noisy parts, concatenation can introduce this noise into the language model's input, potentially affecting the quality of the generated response.

Code Example: Concatenation in Python

Here's a simple example of how you might implement concatenation in Python:

Python

```python
def generate_response(query, retrieved_context):
    """Generates a response using concatenation.

    Args:
        query: The user's query.
        retrieved_context: The context retrieved from the knowledge source.

    Returns:
        A string containing the generated response.
    """
```

```
# Concatenate the query and retrieved context
input_text = f"{query} {retrieved_context}"

# Generate a response using a language model
(replace with your actual LLM)
response = language_model.generate(input_text)

return response
```

This function takes the user's query and the retrieved context as input and concatenates them into a single string. This string is then used as input for the language model to generate a response.

Real-World Examples

Concatenation is used in various RAG applications, especially when dealing with short and concise retrieved information:

- Simple question answering: For questions that can be answered with a short phrase or sentence, concatenation can be an effective way to provide the language model with the necessary context.
- Fact verification: Concatenation can be used to verify the accuracy of a statement by combining it with relevant information from a knowledge source.
- Text summarization: Concatenation can be used to summarize a long document by combining its key sentences or paragraphs.

By understanding the benefits and limitations of concatenation, you can make informed decisions about when to use this technique in your RAG systems. It's a simple yet powerful tool that can be effective for certain applications, especially when combined with other techniques to address its limitations.

3.2.2 Attention-based Fusion

With concatenation, we simply throw all the retrieved information at the language model without any guidance. It's like giving someone a whole book to read when they only need a specific paragraph.

Attention mechanisms, on the other hand, allow the language model to focus on the most relevant parts of the retrieved information. It's like having a highlighter that automatically highlights the most important sentences in a document.

How Does Attention Work in RAG?

In the context of RAG, attention mechanisms work by assigning weights to different parts of the retrieved information. These weights indicate how relevant each part is to the user's query or prompt. The language model then uses these weights to focus its attention on the most important parts of the information.

Think of it like this: you're reading a news article about a specific event. You might skim through the article, paying more attention to the paragraphs that directly relate to the event and less attention to the background information or unrelated details. Attention mechanisms do something similar for language models.

Types of Attention Mechanisms

There are different types of attention mechanisms, but one of the most common ones is called "scaled dot-product attention." It involves calculating the dot product between the query embedding and the embeddings of each part of the retrieved information. These dot products are then scaled and normalized to produce the attention weights.

Benefits of Attention-based Fusion

Attention-based fusion offers several advantages over concatenation:

- Focus on relevant information: It allows the language model to focus on the most relevant parts of the retrieved information, improving the accuracy and relevance of the generated response.
- Handling of long contexts: It can handle long retrieved contexts more effectively than concatenation, as it doesn't require the entire context to be fed to the language model at once.
- Robustness to noise: It can be more robust to noise in the retrieved information, as it can learn to ignore irrelevant or misleading parts.
- Explainability: It can provide insights into the model's reasoning process by revealing which parts of the retrieved information it focused on.

Code Example: Attention-based Fusion with Transformers

Many modern language models, such as those based on the Transformer architecture, have built-in attention mechanisms. Here's a simplified example of how you might use attention-based fusion with a Transformer model in Python:

Python

```python
import torch

from transformers import AutoModelForSeq2SeqLM

# Load a pre-trained Transformer model

model_name = "t5-base"
```

```
model =
AutoModelForSeq2SeqLM.from_pretrained(model_name)

# Prepare the input sequence (query + retrieved
context)

input_ids = tokenizer(input_text,
return_tensors="pt").input_ids

# Generate the response with attention

outputs = model.generate(input_ids,
output_attentions=True)

# Access the attention weights

attentions = outputs.attentions

# Analyze the attention weights to see which
parts of the context the model focused on

# ...
```

In this example, we load a pre-trained Transformer model and generate a response using the generate method. By setting output_attentions=True, we can access the attention weights and analyze them to understand how the model used the retrieved context.

Real-World Examples

Attention-based fusion is used in various RAG applications, including:

- Complex question answering: For questions that require reasoning over multiple sentences or paragraphs, attention mechanisms can help the language model focus on the most relevant parts of the retrieved information.

- Document summarization: Attention mechanisms can help the language model identify the most important sentences in a document and generate a concise summary.
- Dialogue systems: Attention mechanisms can help the model track the conversation history and generate responses that are relevant to the current context.
- Code generation: Attention mechanisms can help the model focus on the relevant parts of the codebase when generating code snippets.

By understanding the principles of attention-based fusion and leveraging the capabilities of Transformer models, you can create more sophisticated and effective RAG systems that can handle complex tasks and long contexts with greater accuracy and efficiency.

3.3 Handling Noise and Irrelevant Retrievals

Sometimes, our retrieval system might not find the perfect information for every query. We might end up with irrelevant documents, outdated information, or even contradictory statements. It's like searching for a recipe online and finding a bunch of websites with different versions, some of which might be inaccurate or incomplete.

This "noise" can throw off our language model and lead to inaccurate or nonsensical outputs. So, how do we deal with this challenge? How do we make our RAG systems more robust and reliable, even when faced with imperfect retrieval?

Strategies for Handling Noise

Fortunately, there are several strategies we can employ to mitigate the impact of noise and irrelevant retrievals:

1. Filtering: Cleaning Up the Input

One approach is to try to clean up the retrieved information before it even reaches the language model. This is like washing the vegetables before cooking – you're removing the dirt and debris to ensure a cleaner and tastier meal.

We can use various filtering techniques to identify and remove irrelevant or low-quality documents. This could involve:

- Heuristics: Simple rules or patterns that can identify potentially irrelevant documents. For example, we might filter out documents that are too short, too old, or that don't contain any of the keywords in the query.
- Machine learning models: We can train machine learning models to classify documents as relevant or irrelevant based on various features, such as their content, source, or metadata.
- Human feedback: We can involve humans in the filtering process, asking them to review the retrieved documents and identify any irrelevant or inaccurate ones.

2. Robust Fusion Techniques

Another approach is to use fusion techniques that are more robust to noise. This is like using a cooking method that can handle slightly imperfect ingredients – you're making the process more forgiving.

For example, attention mechanisms, which we discussed earlier, can help the language model focus on the relevant parts of the retrieved text, even if there is some noise present. It's like being able to pick out the good parts of a dish even if some of the ingredients aren't perfect.

3. Post-processing: Refining the Output

Finally, we can also use post-processing techniques to clean up the generated output. This is like adding some finishing touches to your dish – you're making it look and taste even better.

This could involve:

- Removing inconsistencies: If the generated text contains contradictory statements or inconsistencies, we can use logic or reasoning to identify and remove them.
- Correcting errors: We can use spell checkers, grammar checkers, or even fact-checking tools to correct any errors in the generated text.
- Generating multiple outputs: We can generate multiple outputs from the language model and then use a selection mechanism to choose the best one. This can help to reduce the impact of noise by providing a wider range of options.

Real-World Examples

Handling noise and irrelevant retrievals is crucial in various RAG applications:

- Open-domain question answering: When answering questions based on a large and diverse knowledge source like the web, it's inevitable to encounter some noise and irrelevant information. Robust retrieval and fusion techniques are essential to ensure accurate and reliable answers.
- Summarizing news articles: News articles can contain conflicting information or biased perspectives. Using filtering and post-processing techniques can help to generate more objective and balanced summaries.
- Generating code from natural language: When generating code from natural language descriptions, it's important to handle ambiguity and noise in the input to ensure that the generated code is correct and functional.

Code Example: Filtering with a Simple Heuristic

Here's a simple example of how you might use a heuristic to filter out short documents in Python:

Python

```
def filter_short_documents(documents, min_length=50):
    """Filters out documents that are shorter than a minimum length.

    Args:

        documents: A list of documents, where each document is a string.

        min_length: The minimum length of a document (in characters).

    Returns:

        A list of documents that meet the minimum length requirement.
    """

    filtered_documents = [doc for doc in documents if len(doc) >= min_length]

    return filtered_documents
```

This function takes a list of documents and a minimum length as input and returns a new list containing only the documents that meet the length requirement.

This is a very basic example, of course. In a real-world application, you would likely use more sophisticated heuristics or machine learning models to filter out irrelevant or noisy documents.

By combining these strategies and adapting them to your specific needs, you can make your RAG systems more robust and reliable, even in the face of noisy or imperfect retrieval. This will help you build more trustworthy and effective applications that can truly leverage the power of language models and external knowledge sources.

Chapter 4: Advanced Techniques in RAG

This is where we start to push the boundaries of what RAG can do, exploring more sophisticated approaches to improve accuracy, efficiency, and control. Think of it like leveling up your RAG skills – we're going beyond the basics to master some truly powerful techniques.

4.1 Multi-Step Retrieval

We've mostly talked about retrieval as a single-step process: you have a query, you search your knowledge source, and you retrieve some relevant information. But what if we could make this process more iterative and refined? That's the idea behind multi-step retrieval. It's like searching for something online and then refining your search based on the initial results – you're getting closer to what you're looking for with each step.

4.1.1 Iterative Retrieval and Query Reformulation

Iterative retrieval and query reformulation is where we start to treat retrieval as a more dynamic and interactive process, rather than just a one-shot search.

Think of it like this: you're trying to find a specific item in a large store. You might start by asking a salesperson for general directions, but then you might need to ask more specific questions or look in different aisles based on their initial guidance. You're essentially refining your search strategy as you go along.

That's the essence of iterative retrieval and query reformulation. We start with an initial query, retrieve some documents, analyze the results, and then refine our query based on that analysis. This process can be repeated multiple times until we're satisfied with the retrieved information.

The Iterative Process

Let's break down the iterative retrieval and query reformulation process step by step:

1. **Initial Retrieval:** We start with an initial query, which could be a user's question or a task description. We use this query to search our knowledge source and retrieve a set of documents.
2. **Analysis of Results:** We analyze the retrieved documents to identify potential issues or areas for improvement. This could involve:
    - Relevance assessment: Checking how relevant the retrieved documents are to the query.
    - Diversity assessment: Checking if the retrieved documents cover a diverse range of perspectives or aspects of the topic.
    - Redundancy assessment: Checking if there are any redundant or duplicate documents.
    - Gap analysis: Identifying any missing information or gaps in the retrieved knowledge.
3. **Query Reformulation:** Based on the analysis, we reformulate the query to address the identified issues. This could involve:
    - Query expansion: Adding synonyms or related terms to the query to broaden the search.
    - Query specialization: Making the query more specific by adding constraints or filters to narrow down the search.
    - Query relaxation: Making the query more general by removing constraints or filters to broaden the search.

- o Using feedback: Incorporating user feedback to refine the query based on their specific needs and preferences.
4. **Iteration:** We repeat the retrieval process with the reformulated query. This might involve retrieving a new set of documents or re-ranking the existing documents based on the new query. We continue iterating through these steps until we're satisfied with the retrieved information.

Benefits of Iterative Retrieval and Query Reformulation

This iterative approach offers several benefits:

- Improved accuracy: By refining the query based on the initial results, we can improve the accuracy of the retrieval and find more relevant information.
- Enhanced coverage: By iteratively expanding or specializing the query, we can ensure that we cover a wider range of relevant information.
- Reduced redundancy: By identifying and removing redundant documents, we can improve the efficiency of the retrieval process.
- Adaptation to complex queries: Iterative retrieval is particularly useful for complex or ambiguous queries, where the initial retrieval might not be perfect.

Real-World Examples

Iterative retrieval and query reformulation are used in various applications:

- Academic research: Researchers often use iterative search strategies to find relevant papers and articles. They might start with a broad search and then refine their query based on the initial findings.

- Patent search: Patent examiners use iterative search techniques to find prior art that is relevant to a patent application. They might start with a keyword search and then refine their query based on the initial results and their understanding of the invention.
- Legal research: Lawyers use iterative search strategies to find relevant case law and statutes. They might start with a broad search and then refine their query based on the specific facts and legal issues of their case.

Code Example: Query Expansion in Python

Here's a simple example of how you might implement query expansion in Python:

```python
import nltk
from nltk.corpus import wordnet
def expand_query(query):
    """Expands a query by adding synonyms.
    Args:
      query: The original query string.

    Returns:
      An expanded query string with synonyms.
    """
    # Download WordNet data (if not already downloaded)
    nltk.download('wordnet')
    expanded_query = query
```

```
    for word in query.split():
        for syn in wordnet.synsets(word):
            for lemma in syn.lemmas():
                expanded_query += f" {lemma.name()}"
    return expanded_query
# Example usage
query = "effects of climate change"
expanded_query = expand_query(query)
print(expanded_query)
```

This code defines a function expand_query that takes a query string as input and expands it by adding synonyms from WordNet. This expanded query can then be used for the next iteration of retrieval.

This is a basic example, of course. In a real-world application, you would likely use more sophisticated techniques for query expansion, such as using domain-specific knowledge or learning from user interactions.

By understanding the principles of iterative retrieval and query reformulation and experimenting with different techniques, you can significantly improve the accuracy and efficiency of your RAG systems, especially when dealing with complex or ambiguous queries.

4.2 Contextualized Retrieval

Contextualized retrieval is where we start to make our retrieval systems more aware of the surrounding context, just like we humans use our past experiences and knowledge to understand the present. It's like having a conversation with someone and remembering what you've already talked about – you don't start from scratch each time; you build upon the previous interactions.

In the context of RAG, contextualized retrieval means taking into account the context of the conversation or task when retrieving information. This can significantly improve the relevance and coherence of the retrieved information and ultimately lead to better responses from the language model.

Why Context Matters

Think about it this way: if a user asks, "What are the side effects of aspirin?" and then follows up with "Is it safe for children?", you wouldn't want your retrieval system to treat these questions in isolation. You would want it to remember that the user is asking about aspirin and retrieve information specifically about aspirin and children, not just general information about medication safety for children.

That's where contextualized retrieval comes in. It allows the retrieval system to understand the connections between different queries and retrieve information that is relevant to the overall conversation or task.

Techniques for Contextualized Retrieval

So, how do we actually implement contextualized retrieval? Here are a few techniques:

Maintaining a Conversation History:

- One of the most common approaches is to maintain a history of the conversation. This could be a simple list of previous queries and responses or a more sophisticated representation of the conversation flow.
- By keeping track of the conversation history, the retrieval system can use this information to guide the retrieval process for subsequent queries. For example, it can identify keywords or concepts that have been mentioned earlier and prioritize documents that contain those terms.

Modeling User Preferences:

- Another approach is to model the user's preferences and interests over time. This could involve creating user profiles that capture their past interactions, feedback, and preferences.
- By understanding the user's preferences, the retrieval system can personalize the retrieval results and provide more relevant information. For example, if a user has previously shown interest in a particular topic, the system can prioritize documents related to that topic.

Using External Knowledge:

- We can also incorporate external knowledge about the user, the task, or the domain to guide the retrieval process. This could involve using knowledge graphs, ontologies, or other external resources to understand the relationships between different concepts and entities.
- For example, if a user is asking questions about a specific historical event, the retrieval system could use a knowledge graph to identify related events, people, and places and retrieve information that is relevant to the broader historical context.

Real-World Examples

Contextualized retrieval is used in various applications:

- Dialogue systems: Chatbots and virtual assistants use contextualized retrieval to maintain context and generate coherent responses in multi-turn conversations.
- Personalized search: Search engines use contextualized retrieval to personalize search results based on the user's search history, location, and other factors.

- Question answering: Question answering systems use contextualized retrieval to understand the relationships between different questions and provide more comprehensive answers.
- Recommender systems: Recommender systems use contextualized retrieval to provide recommendations that are relevant to the user's current context and preferences.

Code Example: Using Conversation History in Python

Here's a simplified example of how you might use conversation history to guide retrieval in Python:

Python

```python
def contextualized_retrieval(query, conversation_history):

    """Performs contextualized retrieval based on conversation history.

    Args:

        query: The current query string.

        conversation_history: A list of previous queries and responses.

    Returns:

        A list of retrieved documents.

    """
```

```
# Extract keywords from the conversation history

    keywords = []

    for turn in conversation_history:

        keywords.extend(turn["query"].split())

        keywords.extend(turn["response"].split())

    # Use the keywords to guide the retrieval process

    # (replace with your actual retrieval logic)

    retrieved_documents = retrieve_documents(query, keywords)

    return retrieved_documents
```

This function takes the current query and the conversation history as input. It extracts keywords from the conversation history and uses them to guide the retrieval process. This is a basic example, and you would likely use more sophisticated techniques in a real-world application.

By understanding the principles of contextualized retrieval and implementing some of these techniques, you can significantly improve the relevance and coherence of your RAG systems and create more engaging and informative user experiences.

4.3 Personalized Retrieval

Let's take the idea of contextualized retrieval a step further and talk about personalized retrieval. This is where we really start to tailor the retrieval process to the individual user, making it feel like the system truly understands their needs and preferences. It's like having a personal shopper who knows your style and can pick out the perfect clothes for you, or a music streaming service that recommends songs you'll love based on your listening history.

In the context of RAG, personalized retrieval means going beyond just considering the current context and actually taking into account the user's individual characteristics, interests, and preferences. This can lead to more relevant, engaging, and satisfying user experiences.

Why Personalization Matters

Think about it this way: if two users ask the same question, "What are the best restaurants in Lagos?", they might be looking for very different answers. One user might be a foodie looking for fine dining experiences, while the other might be a tourist looking for budget-friendly local cuisine.

Personalized retrieval allows the system to understand these individual differences and tailor the results accordingly. It's like having a search engine that knows you personally and can provide results that are truly relevant to your needs and interests.

Techniques for Personalized Retrieval

So, how do we actually personalize the retrieval process? Here are a few techniques:

- **Building User Profiles:** One of the key techniques is to build user profiles. These profiles can store various information about the user, such as:
    - Demographics: Age, gender, location, etc.

- Interests: Topics, hobbies, preferences, etc.
- Knowledge level: Expertise in specific domains.
- Interaction history: Past queries, clicks, feedback, etc.

These profiles can be created explicitly through user input or implicitly through analyzing their interactions with the system.

- **Tracking User Interactions:** Another important technique is to continuously track the user's interactions with the system. This could involve:
  - Query logs: Keeping track of the user's past queries.
  - Click-through data: Recording which documents the user clicked on in the search results.
  - Feedback: Collecting explicit feedback from the user on the relevance of the retrieved information.

This interaction data can be used to refine the user profiles and improve the personalization over time.

- **Using Collaborative Filtering:** Collaborative filtering is a technique that leverages the preferences of other users to make recommendations. It's based on the idea that if two users have similar preferences in the past, they are likely to have similar preferences in the future.[1]

In the context of personalized retrieval, we can use collaborative filtering to recommend documents that are similar to those that other users with similar profiles have found relevant.

Real-World Examples

Personalized retrieval is used in various applications:

- Personalized news feeds: News aggregators use personalized retrieval to show users news articles that are relevant to their interests and preferences.
- E-commerce recommendations: E-commerce websites use personalized retrieval to recommend products that are likely to appeal to individual users.
- Personalized learning platforms: Educational platforms use personalized retrieval to recommend learning materials that are tailored to the student's knowledge level and learning goals.
- Personalized search: Search engines use personalized retrieval to provide search results that are relevant to the user's search history, location, and other personal factors.

Code Example: Incorporating User Preferences in Python

Here's a simplified example of how you might incorporate user preferences into the retrieval process in Python:

Python

```
def personalized_retrieval(query, user_profile):

    """Performs personalized retrieval based on user profile.

    Args:

        query: The current query string.

        user_profile: A dictionary containing user preferences.

    Returns:

        A list of retrieved documents.

    """
```

```
    # Extract user interests from the profile
    interests = user_profile.get("interests", [])
    # Use the interests to guide the retrieval
process
    # (replace with your actual retrieval logic)
    retrieved_documents = retrieve_documents(query,
interests)
    return retrieved_documents
```

This function takes the current query and the user profile as input. It extracts the user's interests from the profile and uses them to guide the retrieval process. This is a basic example, and you would likely use more sophisticated techniques in a real-world application.

By understanding the principles of personalized retrieval and implementing some of these techniques, you can create RAG systems that truly cater to the individual needs and preferences of your users, leading to more engaging and satisfying experiences.

4.4 Reinforcement Learning for RAG

Reinforcement learning (RL) is where we start to treat our RAG system as an agent that can learn and adapt over time, kind of like training a pet to do tricks. You reward them for good behavior, and they learn to repeat those actions.

In the context of RAG, we can use reinforcement learning to optimize both the retrieval and generation components of our system. It's like having a self-learning system that constantly improves its performance based on feedback and experience.

How Does Reinforcement Learning Work in RAG?

Let's break down the key elements of reinforcement learning in RAG:

- Agent: This is the part of the RAG system that we want to train. It could be the retrieval component, the generation component, or even the entire system as a whole.
- Environment: This is everything outside the agent. It could include the user, the knowledge source, or a simulated environment that mimics real-world interactions.
- Actions: These are the things the agent can do. For the retrieval component, actions might include selecting documents from the knowledge source. For the generation component, actions might include choosing words or phrases to generate text.
- Rewards: These are signals that tell the agent how well it's doing. We can define rewards based on various factors, such as the relevance of the retrieved documents, the accuracy of the generated text, and the user's satisfaction.

The basic idea of reinforcement learning is to have the agent interact with the environment, take actions, and receive rewards. The agent then learns to adjust its behavior to maximize the rewards it receives over time.

Think of it like this: you're teaching a dog to fetch a ball. You throw the ball, and the dog might run in the wrong direction or chase a butterfly instead. But when the dog finally brings the ball back, you give it a treat (a reward). Over time, the dog learns to associate fetching the ball with getting a treat, and it becomes more likely to repeat that behavior.

Similarly, in RAG, we can reward the agent for retrieving relevant documents, generating accurate responses, and satisfying the user's information needs. The agent then learns to improve its retrieval and generation strategies to maximize these rewards.

Benefits of Reinforcement Learning for RAG

Reinforcement learning offers several advantages for RAG:

- Adaptability: RL allows the RAG system to adapt to changing user needs and preferences over time. It can learn to personalize the retrieval and generation process based on individual user interactions.
- Optimization: RL can optimize the overall performance of the RAG system by finding the best combination of retrieval and generation strategies.
- Handling complex tasks: RL can be particularly useful for complex tasks where it's difficult to define explicit rules or heuristics. The agent can learn to solve the task through trial and error, guided by the reward signals.

Challenges of Reinforcement Learning for RAG

However, there are also some challenges associated with using RL for RAG:

- Reward design: Designing an effective reward function can be challenging. We need to carefully consider what factors are important for success and how to quantify them.
- Exploration-exploitation trade-off: The agent needs to balance exploration (trying new actions) with exploitation (using the actions that have worked well in the past). Finding the right balance can be tricky.
- Computational cost: RL can be computationally expensive, especially for complex tasks and large knowledge sources.

Real-World Examples

Reinforcement learning is being explored in various RAG applications:

- Dialogue systems: RL can be used to train chatbots to have more engaging and informative conversations.
- Recommender systems: RL can be used to personalize recommendations and improve user satisfaction.
- Question answering: RL can be used to train question answering systems to provide more accurate and comprehensive answers.

Code Example: Simple RL for Document Ranking in Python

Here's a simplified example of how you might use reinforcement learning to rank documents in Python:

```python
import random

def rank_documents(query, documents):
    """Ranks documents using a simple reinforcement learning agent.

    Args:

        query: The user's query.

        documents: A list of documents.

    Returns:

        A list of documents ranked by relevance.
    """

    # Initialize the agent (replace with your actual RL agent)
    agent = SimpleRLAgent()
```

```
# Rank the documents
ranked_documents = agent.rank(query, documents)

# Get feedback from the user (replace with your actual feedback mechanism)
feedback = get_user_feedback(ranked_documents)

# Update the agent based on the feedback
agent.update(feedback)

return ranked_documents
```

This code defines a function rank_documents that uses a simple reinforcement learning agent to rank documents. The agent takes the query and documents as input and produces a ranked list. The system then gets feedback from the user and updates the agent based on that feedback. This is a very basic example, and you would likely use a more sophisticated RL algorithm and feedback mechanism in a real-world application.

By understanding the principles of reinforcement learning and experimenting with different RL algorithms and reward functions, you can explore the potential of this powerful technique to optimize your RAG systems and create more adaptive and intelligent applications.

Chapter 5: Applications of Retrieval-Augmented Generation

Let's see how this powerful technology is being applied in the real world. It's like having a Swiss Army knife and finally getting to use all its different tools for various tasks. RAG is incredibly versatile and can be used to enhance a wide range of applications. Let's explore some of the most exciting ones!

5.1 Question Answering

Think about all those times you've typed a question into a search engine or asked a virtual assistant for information. Behind the scenes, there's a good chance that RAG is playing a key role in providing you with those answers.

Traditional question answering systems often relied on a limited set of pre-programmed rules or manually curated knowledge bases. This meant they could only answer a narrow range of questions and often struggled with complex or nuanced queries.

RAG changes the game by allowing question answering systems to tap into vast external knowledge sources, like the entire web or specialized databases.[1] This opens up a whole new world of possibilities, enabling these systems to answer a much wider range of questions with greater accuracy and confidence.

How RAG Powers Question Answering

Let's break down how RAG works in a question answering system:

1. Question Analysis: The system first analyzes the user's question to understand its intent and identify the key concepts or entities involved. This might involve natural

language processing techniques like part-of-speech tagging, named entity recognition, and dependency parsing.
2. Retrieval: Based on the question analysis, the system retrieves relevant information from the knowledge source.[2] This could involve searching a database, querying a search engine, or using a specialized retrieval model.
3. Contextualization: The system then contextualizes the retrieved information, taking into account the specific question and any previous interactions with the user.[3] This might involve filtering out irrelevant information, summarizing key points, or identifying the most relevant passages.
4. Answer Generation: Finally, the system uses a language model to generate a natural language answer based on the retrieved and contextualized information.[4] This might involve extracting answers directly from the text, synthesizing information from multiple sources, or generating a completely new answer based on the understanding of the context.

Benefits of RAG for Question Answering

RAG offers several advantages for question answering:

- Increased coverage: RAG allows question answering systems to access and process information from a much wider range of sources, enabling them to answer a broader set of questions.[5]
- Improved accuracy: By grounding the answers in retrieved evidence, RAG can significantly improve the accuracy and reliability of the answers.[6]
- Enhanced explainability: RAG can provide explanations for the answers by highlighting the sources and evidence used to generate them. This increases transparency and trustworthiness.

- Adaptability: RAG-powered systems can adapt to new information and changing user needs by continuously updating their knowledge sources and retrieval strategies.[7]

Real-World Examples

RAG is used in various question answering applications:

- Search engines: Search engines like Google and Bing use RAG to provide direct answers to user queries, often in the form of featured snippets or knowledge panels.[8]
- Virtual assistants: Virtual assistants like Siri, Alexa, and Google Assistant use RAG to answer questions about various topics, from factual knowledge to personal preferences.[9]
- Customer service chatbots: Companies use RAG-powered chatbots to answer customer questions about products, services, or policies.[10]
- Educational platforms: Educational platforms use RAG to provide students with answers to their questions and support their learning process.[11]

Code Example: Building a Simple QA System with Python

Here's a simplified example of how you might build a basic question answering system using RAG in Python:

```python
def answer_question(question, knowledge_source):

    """Answers a question using RAG.

    Args:

        question: The user's question.
```

```
    knowledge_source: A function that retrieves
relevant information.

    Returns:

    A string containing the answer.

    """

    # Retrieve relevant information

    retrieved_context = knowledge_source(question)

    # Generate an answer (replace with your actual
language model)

    answer = language_model.generate(f"Question:
{question}\nContext: {retrieved_context}")

    return answer
```

This function takes a question and a knowledge source function as input. It retrieves relevant information using the knowledge source and then generates an answer using a language model. This is a very basic example, and you would likely use more sophisticated techniques for retrieval, contextualization, and answer generation in a real-world application.

By understanding the principles of RAG and experimenting with different techniques, you can build powerful and versatile question answering systems that can provide accurate, informative, and engaging answers to a wide range of user queries.

5.2 Dialogue Systems and Conversational AI

Dialogue systems and conversational AI is where we start to see RAG truly shine in creating more engaging, informative, and human-like conversational experiences. Think of those chatbots you interact with on websites or those virtual assistants you talk to on your phone – RAG is increasingly powering those interactions.

Traditional dialogue systems often relied on pre-defined rules and scripts, which limited their ability to handle diverse conversations and unexpected user inputs.[1] It's like having a conversation with someone who can only respond with pre-written lines from a play – it quickly becomes repetitive and unnatural.

RAG changes this by allowing dialogue systems to access and process information from vast external knowledge sources.[2] This enables them to have more dynamic and informative conversations, adapting to the user's needs and providing relevant information on the fly.[3] It's like having a conversation with someone who can access the entire internet and use that knowledge to answer your questions and engage in meaningful discussions.

How RAG Enhances Dialogue Systems

Here's how RAG can be integrated into a dialogue system:

1. Contextual Understanding: RAG helps the system understand the context of the conversation by keeping track of previous turns and retrieving relevant information from the knowledge source.[4] This allows the system to maintain coherence and provide responses that are relevant to the ongoing discussion.[5]
2. Information Retrieval: When the user asks a question or requests information, the system can use RAG to retrieve relevant documents or data from the knowledge source.[6]

This could involve searching a database, querying a search engine, or using a specialized retrieval model.
3. Response Generation: The system can then use the retrieved information to generate a natural and informative response.[7] This might involve extracting answers directly from the retrieved text, summarizing key points, or generating a new response based on the understanding of the context.
4. Personalization: RAG can also be used to personalize the conversation by retrieving information that is relevant to the user's interests, preferences, or past interactions.[8] This can make the conversation more engaging and relevant to the individual user.

Benefits of RAG for Dialogue Systems

RAG offers several benefits for dialogue systems:

- Increased engagement: By providing more informative and relevant responses, RAG can make conversations more engaging and interesting for the user.[9]
- Improved accuracy: RAG can improve the accuracy of the information provided in the conversation by grounding the responses in retrieved evidence.[10]
- Enhanced flexibility: RAG allows dialogue systems to handle a wider range of topics and conversation styles by dynamically accessing and processing information from various sources.[11]
- Personalization: RAG can personalize the conversation by taking into account the user's individual preferences and past interactions.[12]

Real-World Examples

RAG is used in various dialogue systems and conversational AI applications:[13]

- Virtual assistants: Virtual assistants like Siri, Alexa, and Google Assistant use RAG to answer questions, provide information, and perform tasks in a conversational manner.[14]
- Customer support chatbots: Companies use RAG-powered chatbots to handle customer inquiries, resolve issues, and provide support in a more efficient and personalized way.[15]
- Social media chatbots: Social media platforms use RAG to create chatbots that can engage in conversations with users, answer questions, and provide recommendations.
- Educational chatbots: Educational institutions use RAG-powered chatbots to provide students with personalized support, answer questions about courses and programs, and guide them through the learning process.[16]

Code Example: Building a Simple Chatbot with Python

Here's a simplified example of how you might build a basic chatbot using RAG in Python:

```
Python

def chatbot(user_input, conversation_history, knowledge_source):

  """Handles a user input in a chatbot conversation.

  Args:

    user_input: The user's message.

    conversation_history: A list of previous turns in the conversation.
```

```
    knowledge_source: A function that retrieves
relevant information.

    Returns:

    A string containing the chatbot's response.

    """

    # Retrieve relevant information

    retrieved_context =
knowledge_source(user_input,
conversation_history)

    # Generate a response (replace with your actual
language model)

    response = language_model.generate(f"Context:
{retrieved_context}\nUser: {user_input}")

    return response
```

This function takes the user's input, the conversation history, and a knowledge source function as input. It retrieves relevant information using the knowledge source and then generates a response using a language model.[17] This is a very basic example, and you would likely use more sophisticated techniques for context management, retrieval, and response generation in a real-world application.

By understanding the principles of RAG and experimenting with different techniques, you can build more engaging, informative, and personalized dialogue systems that can provide valuable conversational experiences for your users.

5.3 Text Summarization

Traditional text summarization techniques often relied on simple heuristics, like selecting the first few sentences of a document or extracting sentences that contain keywords. But these methods often produced summaries that were incomplete, incoherent, or lacked important information.

RAG takes text summarization to the next level by leveraging the power of language models and external knowledge sources. It's like having a super-smart assistant who can read a document, understand its main points, and then write a concise summary that captures the essence of the text.

How RAG Enhances Text Summarization

Here's how RAG can be used for text summarization:

1. Document Analysis: The system first analyzes the document to identify its key topics, themes, and entities. This might involve natural language processing techniques like topic modeling, keyword extraction, and entity recognition.
2. Retrieval: Based on the document analysis, the system retrieves relevant information from external knowledge sources. This could involve searching for related articles, definitions of key terms, or background information on the topic.
3. Contextualization: The system then contextualizes the retrieved information, integrating it with the document's content to create a richer understanding of the text.
4. Summary Generation: Finally, the system uses a language model to generate a concise and informative summary. This might involve extracting key sentences from the document, paraphrasing important information, or generating a new summary based on the understanding of the context.

Benefits of RAG for Text Summarization

RAG offers several benefits for text summarization:

- Improved accuracy: By incorporating external knowledge, RAG can generate more accurate and comprehensive summaries that capture the main points of the document.
- Enhanced coherence: RAG can produce more coherent and readable summaries by leveraging the language model's ability to generate natural language text.
- Adaptability: RAG-powered summarization systems can adapt to different types of documents and summarization tasks by using different retrieval and generation strategies.
- Personalization: RAG can personalize summaries by taking into account the user's interests, preferences, or background knowledge.

Real-World Examples

RAG is used in various text summarization applications:

- News aggregators: News aggregators use RAG to generate summaries of news articles, allowing users to quickly grasp the main points without reading the entire article.
- Scientific literature review: Researchers use RAG to summarize research papers and generate overviews of the current state of knowledge in a specific field.
- Legal document summarization: Legal professionals use RAG to summarize lengthy legal documents, such as contracts and court filings.
- Business intelligence: Companies use RAG to summarize reports, emails, and other business documents to extract key insights and make informed decisions.

Code Example: Building a Simple Summarization System with Python

Here's a simplified example of how you might build a basic text summarization system using RAG in Python:

Python

```python
def summarize_text(document, knowledge_source):

    """Summarizes a text using RAG.

    Args:

        document: The text to be summarized.

        knowledge_source: A function that retrieves relevant information.

    Returns:

        A string containing the summary.

    """

    # Retrieve relevant information

    retrieved_context = knowledge_source(document)

    # Generate a summary (replace with your actual language model)

    summary = language_model.generate(f"Document: {document}\nContext: {retrieved_context}\nSummary:")

    return summary
```

This function takes a document and a knowledge source function as input. It retrieves relevant information using the knowledge source and then generates a summary using a language model. This is a very basic example, and you would likely use more sophisticated techniques for document analysis, retrieval, and summary generation in a real-world application.

5.4 Code Generation and Code Completion

Writing code can be a time-consuming and complex process. Even experienced developers sometimes struggle to remember the exact syntax, find the right libraries, or figure out the best way to implement a specific function.

This is where RAG comes in, bringing the power of language models and external knowledge to the fingertips of developers. It's like having a coding buddy who can instantly access a vast library of code examples, documentation, and best practices, helping you write better code faster.

How RAG Enhances Code Generation and Completion

RAG can be used to enhance various aspects of code generation and completion:

1. Code Completion: As you type code in your editor, RAG-powered tools can suggest relevant completions based on your current context, the programming language you're using, and even your coding style. This can save you time and reduce errors by automatically completing variable names, function calls, and other code elements.
2. Code Generation: RAG can generate entire code snippets or even functions based on natural language descriptions or examples. This is particularly useful for repetitive tasks or when you need to implement a common function but don't remember the exact syntax.

3. Code Retrieval: RAG can help you find relevant code examples or documentation from a vast code repository. This can be useful when you're facing a new problem or trying to learn a new technique.
4. Code Summarization: RAG can summarize code by generating natural language descriptions of its functionality. This can help you understand complex code or quickly grasp the purpose of a function or module.

Benefits of RAG for Code Generation and Completion

RAG offers several benefits for developers:

- Increased productivity: By automating repetitive tasks and providing intelligent suggestions, RAG can significantly boost developer productivity.
- Reduced errors: RAG can help reduce errors by suggesting correct syntax and identifying potential issues in your code.
- Improved code quality: By providing access to best practices and code examples, RAG can help you write cleaner, more efficient, and more maintainable code.
- Faster learning: RAG can help you learn new programming languages or frameworks by providing relevant code examples and documentation.

Real-World Examples

RAG is used in various code generation and completion tools:

- Integrated Development Environments (IDEs): Popular IDEs like Visual Studio Code, IntelliJ IDEA, and PyCharm are incorporating RAG-powered code completion features.
- Code generation plugins: Plugins like GitHub Copilot and Tabnine use RAG to generate code suggestions and complete code snippets in various code editors.

- Code search engines: Code search engines like Sourcegraph and Grepper use RAG to provide more relevant and accurate search results for code examples and documentation.

Code Example: Using a Language Model for Code Completion in Python

Here's a simplified example of how you might use a language model for code completion in Python:

```python
def complete_code(code_snippet, language_model):
    """Completes a code snippet using a language model.

    Args:

        code_snippet: The incomplete code snippet.

        language_model: The language model used for code completion.

    Returns:

        A string containing the completed code snippet.
    """

    # Generate a completion suggestion (replace with your actual language model)
```

```
completion = language_model.generate(f"Complete 
the following code:\n{code_snippet}")

return completion
```

This function takes an incomplete code snippet and a language model as input. It uses the language model to generate a completion suggestion. This is a very basic example, and you would likely use a more sophisticated language model and context handling in a real-world application.

5.5 Other Applications

We've seen how RAG can be applied to question answering, dialogue systems, text summarization, and code generation. But the versatility of RAG doesn't stop there! It's like a universal tool that can be applied to a wide range of tasks and domains. Let's explore some of these other exciting applications where RAG is making a difference.

1. Report Generation

Think about those tedious reports you might have to create at work, pulling data from various sources like spreadsheets, databases, and websites. RAG can automate much of this process, making it faster and easier to generate informative and insightful reports.

By combining information retrieval with language generation, RAG can:

- Gather data: Extract relevant data from different sources, such as financial databases, customer relationship management (CRM) systems, or marketing analytics platforms.

- Analyze data: Identify trends, patterns, and anomalies in the data.
- Generate reports: Create well-structured reports with text, tables, and visualizations that summarize the key findings and insights.

This can be incredibly useful for businesses, researchers, and analysts who need to generate reports regularly.

Real-World Examples:

- Financial reporting: Generating financial reports that summarize key performance indicators (KPIs), analyze market trends, and provide investment recommendations.
- Marketing reports: Creating reports that analyze campaign performance, track customer engagement, and identify opportunities for improvement.
- Scientific reports: Generating reports that summarize research findings, analyze experimental data, and present conclusions.

2. Creative Writing

Even creative writing can benefit from RAG! While we often think of creativity as a purely human endeavor, RAG can actually assist writers in various ways:

- Generating story ideas: RAG can provide writers with inspiration by generating prompts, suggesting plot twists, or creating character profiles.
- Writing dialogue: RAG can help writers create more realistic and engaging dialogue by suggesting lines, generating different speaking styles, or even translating dialogue into different languages.
- Composing poems or song lyrics: RAG can assist in composing poems or song lyrics by suggesting rhymes, generating different poetic forms, or even translating existing poems into different languages.

This can be a valuable tool for writers who are looking for new ideas, struggling with writer's block, or simply want to explore different creative possibilities.

3. Machine Translation

Machine translation has come a long way, but it still faces challenges in accurately capturing the nuances and subtleties of human language. RAG can help improve machine translation by providing the translation model with context and background knowledge.

By retrieving relevant information from parallel corpora, dictionaries, or knowledge graphs, RAG can:

- Resolve ambiguity: Help the model choose the correct translation for words with multiple meanings.
- Capture cultural nuances: Provide the model with cultural context to ensure that the translation is appropriate and accurate.
- Improve fluency: Help the model generate more natural and fluent translations.

This can lead to more accurate, fluent, and culturally appropriate translations.

4. Data Analysis

Data analysis often involves extracting insights from large and complex datasets. RAG can enhance data analysis by providing context and insights from external knowledge sources.

By retrieving relevant information from research papers, news articles, or domain-specific databases, RAG can:

- Identify patterns and trends: Help analysts identify patterns and trends in the data that might not be immediately obvious.

- **Provide explanations:** Offer explanations for observed patterns or anomalies in the data.
- **Generate hypotheses:** Suggest new hypotheses or research directions based on the analysis.

This can lead to more comprehensive and insightful data analysis.

5. Personalized Learning

RAG can be used to create personalized learning experiences by tailoring the content and difficulty level to individual students.

By retrieving information about the student's learning goals, progress, and preferences, RAG can:

- **Recommend relevant learning materials:** Suggest textbooks, articles, or videos that are appropriate for the student's level and interests.
- **Generate personalized exercises:** Create exercises and quizzes that are tailored to the student's strengths and weaknesses.
- **Provide feedback:** Offer personalized feedback on the student's work and suggest areas for improvement.

This can lead to more effective and engaging learning experiences.

Code Example: Generating a Simple Report in Python

Here's a simplified example of how you might use RAG to generate a simple report in Python:

Python

```
def generate_report(data, knowledge_source):

    """Generates a simple report based on data and external knowledge.

    Args:
```

```
    data: The data to be included in the report.

    knowledge_source: A function that retrieves
relevant information.

    Returns:

    A string containing the report.

    """

    # Retrieve relevant context

    retrieved_context = knowledge_source(data)

    # Generate the report (replace with your actual
language model)

    report = language_model.generate(f"Data:
{data}\nContext: {retrieved_context}\nReport:")

    return report
```

This function takes data and a knowledge source function as input. It retrieves relevant context using the knowledge source and then generates a report using a language model. This is a very basic example, and you would likely use more sophisticated techniques for data analysis, retrieval, and report generation in a real-world application.

These are just a few examples of the many ways RAG can be applied to different tasks and domains. As the field continues to evolve, we can expect to see even more innovative and impactful applications emerge. The key is to think creatively about how to combine the power of language models with external knowledge sources to solve real-world problems and create new possibilities.

Chapter 6: Building and Deploying RAG Systems

We've covered a lot of ground exploring the theory and applications of RAG. Now, let's get practical and talk about how to actually build and deploy these systems in the real world. It's like having a blueprint for a cool invention and finally getting to build it and share it with the world.

Building and deploying RAG systems involves a range of considerations, from choosing the right tools and data to ensuring efficiency, scalability, and ethical responsibility. Let's break it down step by step.

6.1 Practical Considerations

Building a successful RAG system requires careful planning and consideration of various factors. Let's break down some of the key practical aspects:

1. Define Your Goals

First and foremost, you need to have a clear understanding of what you want to achieve with your RAG system. What problem are you trying to solve? What are your specific objectives?

Are you building a question answering system that can provide accurate and comprehensive answers to user queries? Are you creating a chatbot that can engage in natural and informative conversations? Or are you developing a text summarization tool that can condense lengthy documents into concise summaries?

Having well-defined goals will guide your design and implementation choices. It will help you choose the right tools, data sources, and evaluation metrics.

2. Identify Your Users

Who will be using your RAG system? What are their needs and expectations? Understanding your users is crucial for creating a system that is truly useful and effective.

Consider factors like:

- User expertise: Are your users experts in the domain, or are they novices? This will influence the complexity and level of detail in your system's responses.
- User goals: What are your users trying to achieve with your system? Are they looking for quick answers, in-depth information, or creative inspiration?
- User preferences: Do your users prefer concise summaries or detailed explanations? Do they prefer visual or textual information?

By understanding your users, you can tailor your RAG system to their specific needs and preferences, creating a more satisfying and engaging experience.

3. Choose Your Knowledge Source

The knowledge source is the foundation of your RAG system. It's the source of information that your system will draw upon to answer questions, generate text, or complete tasks.

Choosing the right knowledge source is crucial for the accuracy, relevance, and comprehensiveness of your system. Consider factors like:

- Data quality: Is the data accurate, complete, and up-to-date?
- Data relevance: Is the data relevant to the task you're trying to solve?
- Data coverage: Does the data cover the range of topics and domains that your system needs to handle?

- Data format: Is the data in a format that is suitable for your retrieval and fusion techniques?
- Data access: Do you have the necessary permissions and access to use the data?

You might choose to use a public knowledge source, like Wikipedia or Common Crawl, or you might create your own private knowledge source based on your own data or curated content.

4. Select Your Language Model

The language model is the engine of your RAG system. It's the component that generates the text, answers the questions, or completes the tasks.

Choosing the right language model is crucial for the performance and efficiency of your system. Consider factors like:

- Model size: Larger models generally have better performance but require more computational resources.
- Model specialization: Some models are specialized for specific tasks, such as question answering or text summarization.
- Model availability: Some models are publicly available, while others require licensing or access through an API.

You might choose to use a pre-trained language model, like GPT-3 or BERT, or you might fine-tune a model on your own data to improve its performance on your specific task.

5. Plan for Evaluation

Evaluation is essential for understanding how well your RAG system is performing and identifying areas for improvement. It's like checking your map and compass during your road trip to make sure you're on the right track.

Plan for evaluation from the start by considering:

- Evaluation metrics: What metrics will you use to measure the performance of your system? This might include accuracy, relevance, fluency, or user satisfaction.
- Evaluation data: What data will you use for evaluation? You might use a held-out portion of your training data or a separate evaluation dataset.
- Evaluation methods: How will you conduct the evaluation? You might use automated metrics, human evaluation, or a combination of both.

By carefully considering these practical aspects, you can lay a solid foundation for building a successful RAG system that meets your goals and satisfies your users. It's all about planning ahead, choosing the right tools and resources, and keeping your users and objectives in mind throughout the process.

6.2 Tools, Libraries, and Frameworks for RAG

Alright, let's get down to the practical side of things and explore the tools and resources that can help you build your own RAG system. It's like setting up a workshop – you need the right tools and equipment to get the job done efficiently and effectively.

Fortunately, the RAG landscape is blossoming with a variety of tools, libraries, and frameworks that can simplify the development process and provide you with powerful building blocks. Let's take a look at some of the most popular ones:

1. LangChain

LangChain is a powerful and versatile framework specifically designed for developing applications powered by large language models. It provides a modular and extensible set of tools for:

- Retrieval: Connecting to various data sources and retrieving relevant information.

- Fusion: Combining retrieved information with user queries or prompts.
- Language Model Interaction: Interacting with different language models, including prompt engineering and response generation.
- Chains: Creating complex workflows by chaining together multiple components.
- Agents: Building autonomous agents that can make decisions and take actions based on language model outputs.

LangChain's modular design makes it easy to customize and adapt to different RAG applications. It also supports a wide range of integrations with other tools and libraries.

Code Example:

```python
from langchain.document_loaders import TextLoader
from langchain.text_splitter import CharacterTextSplitter
from langchain.embeddings import OpenAIEmbeddings
from langchain.vectorstores import FAISS

# Load documents
loader = TextLoader('my_documents.txt')
documents = loader.load()

# Split documents into chunks
```

```
text_splitter =
CharacterTextSplitter(chunk_size=1000,
chunk_overlap=0)

texts = text_splitter.split_documents(documents)³

# Create embeddings and store in a vector
database

embeddings = OpenAIEmbeddings()

db = FAISS.from_documents(texts, embeddings)

# Perform a similarity search

query = "What is the capital of France?"

docs = db.similarity_search(query)

# Print the retrieved documents

print(docs)
```

This code demonstrates a simple RAG pipeline using LangChain. It loads a text document, splits it into chunks, creates embeddings, stores them in a FAISS vector database, and performs a similarity search.

2. Haystack

Haystack is another popular framework for building RAG systems, particularly focused on question answering and semantic search. It provides a comprehensive set of tools for:

- Data Ingestion: Loading data from various sources, including files, databases, and APIs.
- Document Processing: Cleaning, splitting, and preparing documents for indexing.

- Retrieval: Performing dense and sparse retrieval using different retrieval models and techniques.
- Readers: Extracting answers from retrieved documents using different reader models.
- Pipelines: Creating complex QA pipelines by combining different components.
- Evaluation: Evaluating the performance of your QA system using various metrics.

Haystack is particularly well-suited for building production-ready QA systems with features like distributed processing, fault tolerance, and monitoring.

3. FAISS

FAISS (Facebook AI Similarity Search) is a highly efficient library for similarity search and clustering of dense vectors. It's a great choice for dense retrieval in RAG, especially when dealing with large datasets.

FAISS provides a variety of indexing and search methods, including:

- Exact search: Finding the exact nearest neighbors.
- Approximate nearest neighbor (ANN) search: Finding approximate nearest neighbors with high speed and accuracy.
- Product quantization: Compressing vectors to reduce storage and computation costs.

FAISS is optimized for performance and can handle billions of vectors efficiently.

4. Hugging Face Transformers

Hugging Face Transformers is a popular library that provides access to a wide range of pre-trained language models, including BERT, GPT, and RoBERTa. It also provides tools for:

- Fine-tuning: Adapting pre-trained models to specific tasks and datasets.
- Inference: Using models for text generation, question answering, and other tasks.
- Deployment: Deploying models for production use.

Hugging Face Transformers is a valuable resource for building and deploying RAG systems, especially when you need to use state-of-the-art language models.

5. SentenceTransformers

SentenceTransformers is a library that provides pre-trained sentence embedding models that are specifically optimized for semantic similarity tasks. This makes them ideal for dense retrieval in RAG.

SentenceTransformers offers a variety of models based on different architectures, such as BERT, RoBERTa, and DistilBERT. These models can be used to generate high-quality embeddings for sentences, paragraphs, or even entire documents.

Other Tools and Libraries

In addition to these, there are many other tools and libraries that can be useful for building RAG systems, such as:

- spaCy: A powerful library for natural language processing tasks, including tokenization, part-of-speech tagging, and named entity recognition.[4]
- NLTK: Another popular library for natural language processing, offering a wide range of tools and resources.
- Gensim: A library for topic modeling and document similarity analysis.
- Redis: An in-memory data store that can be used for caching and storing embeddings.
- Elasticsearch: A powerful search engine that can be used for indexing and retrieving documents.

By exploring these tools, libraries, and frameworks, you can find the best combination for your specific needs and build powerful and efficient RAG systems.

6.3 Data Sources and Preparation

Just like a car needs the right type of fuel to run smoothly, your RAG system needs the right kind of data to perform effectively. And just like you wouldn't put dirty or contaminated fuel in your car, you need to make sure your data is clean and well-prepared.

Choosing the right data sources and preparing them properly is crucial for the success of your RAG system. Let's break down the key considerations:

1. Identifying Relevant Data Sources

The first step is to identify data sources that are relevant to your RAG application. This depends on the specific task you're trying to solve and the type of information your system needs to access.

Here are a few potential data sources:

- Public Datasets: There are many publicly available datasets that can be used for RAG, covering a wide range of topics and domains. Some popular examples include:
    - Wikipedia: A massive collection of articles on various topics.
    - Common Crawl: A massive dataset of web pages.
    - Hugging Face Datasets: A collection of datasets for natural language processing tasks.
    - Google Dataset Search: A search engine for datasets.
- Private Datasets: You might also have access to private datasets within your organization or through partnerships. These datasets could contain valuable information that is not publicly available.

- APIs: Many online services provide APIs that allow you to access their data programmatically. This could include news APIs, social media APIs, or financial data APIs.
- Web Scraping: If the information you need is not available through public datasets or APIs, you might consider web scraping. This involves extracting data from websites using automated tools. However, be sure to respect website terms of service and robots.txt files.

2. Assessing Data Quality

Once you've identified potential data sources, it's important to assess the quality of the data. Here are some key factors to consider:

- Accuracy: Is the data accurate and free from errors?
- Completeness: Is the data complete and comprehensive?
- Consistency: Is the data consistent in terms of format and terminology?
- Timeliness: Is the data up-to-date and relevant to your current needs?
- Bias: Does the data contain any biases that could affect the performance of your system?

It's important to critically evaluate the data sources and choose those that provide high-quality and reliable information.

3. Data Preparation

Once you have your data sources, you need to prepare the data for use in your RAG system. This might involve:

- Cleaning: Removing any noise, inconsistencies, or errors in the data. This could include:
    - Removing duplicate entries: Identifying and removing duplicate records.

- Correcting typos and inconsistencies: Fixing spelling errors, standardizing capitalization, and ensuring consistent formatting.
- Handling missing values: Deciding how to handle missing data, such as filling in missing values or removing records with missing data.
* Formatting: Converting the data into a format that is suitable for your retrieval and fusion techniques. This might involve:
  - Converting to a standard format: Converting data from various formats (e.g., PDF, HTML, CSV) into a common format, such as JSON.
  - Creating embeddings: Generating embeddings for your data if you're using dense retrieval techniques.
* Structuring: Organizing the data in a way that makes it easy to access and retrieve. This might involve:
  - Creating indexes: Creating indexes on your data to speed up retrieval.
  - Chunking: Dividing large documents into smaller chunks to make them easier to process.

Code Example: Cleaning Text Data in Python

Here's a simple example of how you might clean text data in Python:

```python
import re

def clean_text(text):

    """Cleans text data by removing punctuation and converting to lowercase.

    Args:
```

        text: The text to be cleaned.

    Returns:

        The cleaned text.

    """

    # Remove punctuation

    text = re.sub(r'[^\w\s]', '', text)

    # Convert to lowercase

    text = text.lower()

    return text

Example usage

text = "This is an example text with some punctuation!"

cleaned_text = clean_text(text)

print(cleaned_text) # Output: this is an example text with some punctuation

This code defines a function clean_text that removes punctuation and converts text to lowercase. This is a basic example, and you might need more sophisticated cleaning techniques depending on your data.

Real-World Examples

Data preparation is crucial in various RAG applications:

- **Question answering:** Cleaning and formatting Wikipedia articles to create a knowledge source for a question answering system.
- **Chatbots:** Preparing a company's internal knowledge base for use in a customer service chatbot.
- **Text summarization:** Chunking long documents into smaller segments for summarization.

By carefully choosing your data sources, assessing their quality, and preparing them properly, you can ensure that your RAG system has access to the high-quality information it needs to perform effectively.

6.4 Efficiency and Scalability

Let's talk about making your RAG system run like a well-oiled machine. It's not just about getting the right answers; it's about getting them quickly and efficiently, even when dealing with tons of data and a constant stream of requests. This is where efficiency and scalability come into play.

Think of it like building a bridge – you don't just want it to stand; you want it to handle heavy traffic and withstand strong winds. Similarly, your RAG system needs to be built to handle large amounts of data and a high volume of queries without slowing down or crashing.

Why Efficiency and Scalability Matter

Efficiency and scalability are crucial for several reasons:

- User experience: No one likes to wait for ages to get an answer or see a spinning wheel while a system struggles to

process a request. Efficient systems provide a smooth and responsive user experience.
- Cost-effectiveness: Inefficient systems can consume a lot of computational resources, leading to higher costs for hardware, energy, and maintenance. Scalable systems can handle increasing workloads without requiring a proportional increase in resources.
- Real-world applicability: Many real-world applications require RAG systems to handle massive datasets and high query volumes. For example, a search engine needs to be able to process millions of queries per second and retrieve relevant information from billions of web pages.

Techniques for Efficiency and Scalability

Here are some key techniques you can use to optimize your RAG system for efficiency and scalability:

1. Efficient Retrieval

The retrieval component is often the bottleneck in a RAG system, as it involves searching through a large knowledge source. To optimize retrieval, you can use techniques like:

- Approximate Nearest Neighbor (ANN) Search: For dense retrieval, ANN search algorithms like FAISS can significantly speed up the search process by finding approximate nearest neighbors instead of exact ones.
- Inverted Indexes: For sparse retrieval, inverted indexes can efficiently locate documents that contain specific keywords.
- Caching: Caching frequently accessed data or embeddings can avoid redundant computations and speed up retrieval.

2. Efficient Fusion

The fusion component combines the retrieved information with the user query or prompt. To optimize fusion, you can:

- Use efficient attention mechanisms: Attention mechanisms can be computationally expensive. Choose efficient implementations or consider alternatives like sparse attention.
- Optimize the input sequence length: Limit the amount of retrieved context included in the input sequence to avoid exceeding the language model's capacity.

3. Language Model Optimization

The language model itself can also be optimized for efficiency:

- Use smaller models: Consider using smaller language models or distilled versions of larger models if they can achieve sufficient performance for your task.
- Quantization: Quantize the model's weights to reduce their size and speed up computations.
- Pruning: Remove unnecessary connections or parameters in the model to reduce its complexity.

4. System-Level Optimization

In addition to optimizing individual components, you can also optimize the system as a whole:

- Asynchronous processing: Handle requests asynchronously to avoid blocking the system while waiting for long-running tasks to complete.
- Load balancing: Distribute the workload across multiple machines to handle high query volumes.
- Database optimization: Optimize your database for efficient storage and retrieval of data and embeddings.

Code Example: Using FAISS for Efficient Similarity Search

Here's an example of how you might use FAISS to perform efficient similarity search in Python:

Python

```python
import numpy as np

import faiss

# Generate some random vectors

dimension = 128

num_vectors = 1000000

vectors = np.random.rand(num_vectors, dimension).astype('float32')

# Create a FAISS index (using IndexIVFFlat for approximate nearest neighbor search)

quantizer = faiss.IndexFlatL2(dimension)

index = faiss.IndexIVFFlat(quantizer, dimension, 100)

index.train(vectors)

index.add(vectors)

# Create a query vector
```

```
query_vector = np.random.rand(1,
dimension).astype('float32')

# Search for the nearest neighbors

k = 5

D, I = index.search(query_vector, k)

# Print the indices of the nearest neighbors

print(I)
```

This code demonstrates how to create a FAISS index and use it for efficient similarity search. FAISS provides various indexing options and parameters that you can tune to optimize performance for your specific dataset and requirements.

Real-World Examples

Efficiency and scalability are crucial in many RAG applications:

- Search engines: Search engines need to handle millions of queries per second efficiently.
- Chatbots: Chatbots need to respond to user requests quickly and maintain context in long conversations.
- Recommendation systems: Recommendation systems need to process large amounts of user data and provide personalized recommendations in real-time.

By carefully considering these techniques and applying them to your RAG system, you can ensure that it can handle real-world demands and provide a smooth and responsive user experience.

6.5 Ethical Considerations in RAG

RAG systems, with their ability to access and process vast amounts of information, have the potential to be incredibly powerful and beneficial. But they also come with ethical considerations that we need to address to ensure they are used for good and avoid unintended consequences.

1. Bias

One of the biggest ethical concerns with RAG is bias. Language models are trained on massive amounts of data, and this data can reflect and amplify existing biases in society. If we're not careful, our RAG systems can perpetuate these biases, leading to unfair or discriminatory outcomes.

For example, if a RAG system is trained on data that contains gender stereotypes, it might generate responses that reinforce those stereotypes. Or if a system is trained on data that is predominantly from one culture, it might not be able to accurately understand or respond to queries from other cultures.

Mitigating Bias:

- Data diversity: Ensure that your training data is diverse and representative of different groups and perspectives.
- Bias detection and mitigation: Use techniques to detect and mitigate bias in your data and models.
- Fairness metrics: Evaluate your system's performance on different groups to ensure it's not unfairly biased against any particular group.

2. Privacy

RAG systems often deal with sensitive information, such as personal data, medical records, or financial information. It's crucial to protect user privacy and ensure that your system handles this data responsibly.

This means:

- Data security: Implement strong security measures to protect data from unauthorized access or breaches.
- Data anonymization: Anonymize or pseudonymous personal data whenever possible.
- Transparency: Be transparent with users about what data you collect and how you use it.
- Compliance: Comply with relevant privacy regulations, such as GDPR or CCPA.

3. Transparency

Transparency is key to building trust and accountability in RAG systems. Users should be able to understand how the system works, what data it uses, and how it arrives at its answers or recommendations.

This means:

- Explainability: Provide explanations for the system's outputs, highlighting the sources and evidence used to generate them.
- Documentation: Clearly document the system's architecture, data sources, and algorithms.
- User control: Give users control over their data and allow them to opt out of data collection or personalization.

4. Misinformation

RAG systems can sometimes generate incorrect or misleading information, especially when dealing with complex or ambiguous queries. This can have serious consequences, especially in domains like healthcare or finance.

To mitigate this risk:

- Fact-checking: Incorporate fact-checking mechanisms to verify the accuracy of the retrieved information.
- Hallucination detection: Use techniques to detect and mitigate hallucinations or generated content that deviates from the retrieved information.
- Source attribution: Clearly attribute the sources of information used in the system's outputs.

5. Accountability

It's important to establish clear lines of accountability for the decisions and actions of RAG systems. Who is responsible if the system makes a mistake or causes harm?

This involves:

- Human oversight: Ensure that there is human oversight of the system's operation and that humans can intervene if necessary.
- Auditing: Regularly audit the system's performance and identify any potential issues or biases.
- Ethical guidelines: Develop clear ethical guidelines for the development and deployment of RAG systems.

Real-World Examples

Ethical considerations are crucial in various RAG applications:

- Healthcare: Ensuring that medical advice provided by a RAG system is accurate, unbiased, and respects patient privacy.
- Finance: Preventing a financial RAG system from making biased investment recommendations or misusing personal financial data.
- News and media: Ensuring that RAG-powered news summarization systems do not spread misinformation or amplify harmful biases.

By carefully considering these ethical aspects and taking proactive steps to address them, you can build and deploy RAG systems that are not only powerful and effective but also responsible and ethical.

Chapter 7: Future Directions of RAG

We've journeyed through the core concepts, techniques, and applications of RAG. Now, let's look ahead to the future! It's like reaching the end of a map and wondering what lies beyond the horizon. The field of RAG is constantly evolving, with new research and developments emerging all the time. Let's explore some of the exciting trends and challenges that are shaping the future of this technology.

7.1 Emerging Trends and Research

Let's take a peek into the exciting world of emerging trends and research in RAG. It's like being at the forefront of innovation, where new ideas and discoveries are constantly shaping the future of this technology.

The field of RAG is dynamic and rapidly evolving, with researchers exploring new frontiers and pushing the boundaries of what's possible. Let's explore some of the most promising trends and research directions:

1. Neuro-symbolic AI

This is a fascinating area of research that aims to bridge the gap between two powerful approaches to AI: neural networks and symbolic AI.

Neural networks, like those used in language models, are great at learning patterns and relationships from data, but they often struggle with reasoning and logic. Symbolic AI, on the other hand, excels at logic and reasoning but can be brittle and inflexible when faced with real-world complexity.

Neuro-symbolic AI seeks to combine the strengths of both approaches, creating systems that can learn from data and reason about it logically. In the context of RAG, this could lead to systems that can not only retrieve and generate text but also understand the meaning and implications of that information.

For example, a neuro-symbolic RAG system could be used to answer questions that require complex reasoning or to generate explanations that are logically sound and consistent with the retrieved knowledge.

2. Multimodal RAG

Most current RAG systems focus primarily on text. But the world is full of different modalities of information, such as images, audio, and video. Multimodal RAG aims to expand the capabilities of RAG systems to handle these different modalities.

This could involve:

- Retrieving information from multimodal sources: Searching for images, audio clips, or videos that are relevant to a user's query.
- Generating multimodal outputs: Generating responses that include not just text but also images, audio, or video.
- Integrating information from different modalities: Combining information from different modalities to create a more comprehensive understanding of the context.

For example, a multimodal RAG system could be used to answer questions about images, generate captions for videos, or even create multimedia presentations.

3. Interactive Retrieval

Traditional retrieval systems often operate in a single step: the user provides a query, and the system retrieves relevant information. But in many cases, it might be beneficial to have a more interactive retrieval process.

Interactive retrieval involves a back-and-forth exchange between the user and the system. The system might ask clarifying questions, provide intermediate results, or refine its search based on user feedback.

This could lead to more accurate and personalized retrieval experiences, especially for complex or ambiguous queries.

4. Generative Knowledge Bases

Most knowledge bases are static collections of facts and relationships. But what if we could create knowledge bases that are more dynamic and generative?

Generative knowledge bases could:

- Generate new knowledge: Infer new facts or relationships based on existing knowledge.
- Adapt to new information: Update their knowledge based on new data or feedback.
- Provide explanations: Explain the reasoning behind their knowledge or inferences.

This could lead to RAG systems that are more adaptable, informative, and trustworthy.

5. Explainable RAG

As RAG systems become more complex and sophisticated, it's important to make them more transparent and explainable. Users should be able to understand how these systems work and why they make certain decisions.

Explainable RAG research focuses on:

- Providing insights into the retrieval process: Explaining why certain documents were retrieved and others were not.
- Highlighting relevant information: Highlighting the parts of the retrieved information that were used to generate the response.
- Explaining the reasoning process: Providing a step-by-step explanation of how the system arrived at its answer or recommendation.

This can help build trust and accountability in RAG systems.

Real-World Examples and Code Snippets

While some of these research areas are still in their early stages, we can already see glimpses of their potential in real-world applications:

- Multimodal search: Search engines like Google are starting to incorporate multimodal search, allowing users to search for information using images or voice.
- Interactive chatbots: Some chatbots are starting to use interactive retrieval to clarify user requests and provide more relevant responses.

As these trends and research directions continue to develop, we can expect to see even more innovative and impactful applications of RAG in the years to come.

7.2 Challenges and Open Problems

While RAG is a promising approach with many successful applications, it's not without its challenges.[1] It's like climbing a mountain – you might encounter obstacles and unexpected difficulties along the way. The field of RAG is still relatively young, and there are many open problems and research questions that need to be addressed to fully realize its potential.[2]

Let's explore some of these challenges:

1. Scalability

One of the biggest challenges in RAG is scalability.[3] As datasets grow larger and models become more complex, it becomes increasingly difficult to build systems that can efficiently handle massive amounts of data and high query volumes.

Think of it like building a library – as the number of books grows, you need more shelves, more space, and a better organization system to keep everything accessible. Similarly, RAG systems need to be designed to scale efficiently as the amount of data and the number of users increase.[4]

This involves:

- Efficient retrieval: Developing retrieval methods that can quickly find relevant information in massive datasets.[5]
- Optimized data structures: Using data structures like inverted indexes or approximate nearest neighbor search to speed up retrieval.[6]
- Distributed computing: Distributing the workload across multiple machines to handle high query volumes.[7]

2. Adaptability

Another challenge is adaptability. RAG systems often struggle to adapt to new domains or tasks.[8] They might be trained on a specific dataset or for a specific purpose, and their performance can drop significantly when applied to a different domain or task.

It's like learning a new language – you might be fluent in one language, but you need to learn new vocabulary and grammar rules to communicate effectively in another language. Similarly, RAG systems need to be able to adapt to new domains and tasks by learning new concepts and relationships.[9]

This involves:

- Transfer learning: Developing techniques to transfer knowledge from one domain or task to another.[10]
- Domain adaptation: Adapting models to new domains by fine-tuning them on domain-specific data.[11]
- Meta-learning: Learning how to learn, so that the system can quickly adapt to new tasks.[12]

3. Evaluation

Evaluating the performance of RAG systems can be tricky. Traditional metrics like accuracy or precision might not be sufficient to capture the nuanced aspects of retrieval and generation.

It's like judging a painting – you can't just measure its dimensions or count the number of colors used. You need to consider factors like composition, technique, and emotional impact. Similarly, evaluating RAG systems requires considering factors like relevance, coherence, fluency, and user satisfaction.[13]

This involves:

- Developing new evaluation metrics: Creating metrics that can capture the multifaceted aspects of RAG performance.[14]
- Human evaluation: Incorporating human judgment into the evaluation process.[15]
- Benchmark datasets: Creating standardized benchmark datasets for different RAG tasks.

4. Robustness

RAG systems can be vulnerable to noisy or adversarial inputs.[16] Noisy data, incomplete information, or even deliberately misleading queries can throw off the system and lead to inaccurate or nonsensical outputs.[17]

It's like trying to read a map with missing or incorrect information – you might end up getting lost. Similarly, RAG systems need to be robust to noise and adversarial attacks to ensure they provide reliable and trustworthy information.[18]

This involves:

- Noise-resistant retrieval: Developing retrieval methods that can handle noisy or incomplete data.[19]
- Adversarial training: Training models to be resistant to adversarial attacks.[20]
- Error detection and correction: Incorporating mechanisms to detect and correct errors in the retrieved information or generated text.[21]

5. Ethical Considerations

As we discussed earlier, ethical considerations are crucial in the development and deployment of RAG systems. Bias, privacy, misinformation, and accountability are all important issues that need to be addressed.[22]

This involves:

- Developing ethical guidelines: Creating clear guidelines for the responsible development and use of RAG.[23]
- Bias mitigation: Implementing techniques to detect and mitigate bias in data and models.[24]
- Privacy protection: Ensuring that user data is handled responsibly and ethically.[25]
- Misinformation prevention: Taking steps to prevent the generation and spread of misinformation.

By addressing these challenges and continuing to research and develop new solutions, we can unlock the full potential of RAG and create systems that are not only powerful and effective but also ethical, reliable, and beneficial to society.

7.3 The Future of RAG and Language Models

RAG is more than just a cool technique; it represents a fundamental shift in how we think about language models. Instead of viewing them as isolated entities with limited knowledge, we're now starting to see them as bridges to vast external knowledge sources. This opens up a whole new world of possibilities, allowing language models to become more knowledgeable, versatile, and trustworthy.

The Convergence of Retrieval and Generation

The future of RAG is intertwined with the future of language models themselves. As language models become more powerful and sophisticated, they will be able to handle even more complex retrieval and generation tasks.

We can expect to see a tighter integration of retrieval and generation, where the two processes become more intertwined and synergistic. For example, language models might be able to dynamically retrieve information as they generate text, adapting their search strategies based on the evolving context.

This convergence of retrieval and generation will lead to more intelligent and adaptable language models that can truly understand and respond to our needs.

Expanding Applications

As RAG technology matures, we can expect to see it applied to an even wider range of applications. Some areas where RAG is likely to have a significant impact include:

- Personalized Education: RAG can be used to create personalized learning experiences that adapt to individual student needs and learning styles. Imagine AI tutors that

can answer questions, provide feedback, and recommend relevant learning materials based on a student's specific strengths and weaknesses.
- Healthcare: RAG can assist doctors and nurses in diagnosing diseases, recommending treatments, and providing personalized healthcare advice. Imagine AI systems that can analyze patient data, retrieve relevant medical information, and generate comprehensive reports to support clinical decision-making.
- Scientific Discovery: RAG can help researchers analyze scientific literature, identify research gaps, and generate new hypotheses. Imagine AI systems that can sift through thousands of research papers, extract key findings, and suggest new avenues for scientific exploration.
- Creative Industries: RAG can assist artists, writers, and musicians in their creative process. Imagine AI tools that can generate story ideas, compose music, or create artwork based on natural language prompts.

The Rise of Augmented Intelligence

RAG is not just about replacing human intelligence; it's about augmenting it. By providing us with access to vast amounts of information and powerful language processing capabilities, RAG can help us make better decisions, solve complex problems, and unleash our creative potential.

We can envision a future where RAG systems act as our collaborators and partners, helping us navigate the information overload and make sense of the world around us. This is the promise of augmented intelligence – a future where humans and AI work together to achieve more than either could alone.

Ethical and Societal Considerations

As RAG technology becomes more pervasive, it's crucial to address the ethical and societal implications. We need to ensure that these systems are used responsibly, fairly, and transparently.

This involves:

- Developing ethical guidelines: Creating clear guidelines for the development and deployment of RAG systems.
- Promoting fairness and inclusivity: Ensuring that RAG systems do not perpetuate biases or discriminate against certain groups.
- Protecting privacy: Safeguarding user data and ensuring that RAG systems respect privacy.
- Fostering transparency: Making RAG systems transparent and explainable so that users can understand how they work and why they make certain decisions.

By addressing these ethical and societal considerations, we can ensure that RAG technology is used for good and benefits all of humanity.

The future of RAG is full of exciting possibilities and challenges. As we continue to research, develop, and deploy this technology, we need to do so responsibly and ethically, keeping in mind the potential benefits and risks.

By working together, we can shape a future where RAG and language models empower us to achieve more, understand the world better, and create a more just and equitable society.

Conclusion

The discussion of Retrieval-Augmented Generation (RAG) has taken us on a journey through the fascinating intersection of information retrieval and natural language generation. We've seen how RAG empowers language models to tap into vast external knowledge sources, transforming them from static repositories of information into dynamic and adaptable engines of understanding and creation.

We began by examining the limitations of traditional language models, highlighting their struggles with factual accuracy, consistency, and controllability. We then introduced RAG as a powerful solution, demonstrating how it grounds language generation in external knowledge, leading to more reliable, informative, and controllable language technologies.

We delved into the core components of RAG systems, exploring various retrieval methods, fusion techniques, and generation strategies. We examined the intricacies of dense and sparse retrieval, the nuances of concatenation and attention-based fusion, and the power of fine-tuning and prompting.

We ventured beyond the basics, exploring advanced techniques like multi-step retrieval, contextualized retrieval, personalized retrieval, and even the potential of reinforcement learning for RAG. We witnessed how these techniques push the boundaries of what's possible, enabling more sophisticated and adaptive RAG systems.

We surveyed the diverse landscape of RAG applications, witnessing its transformative impact on question answering, dialogue systems, text summarization, code generation, and many other fields. We saw how RAG empowers us to build more intelligent and versatile systems that can answer our questions, generate creative content, and assist us in various tasks.

We also addressed the practical considerations of building and deploying RAG systems, discussing tools, libraries, data sources, efficiency, scalability, and ethical considerations. We emphasized the importance of responsible development and deployment, ensuring that RAG systems are used for good and avoid unintended consequences.

Finally, we peered into the future of RAG, exploring emerging trends and research directions, such as neuro-symbolic AI, multimodal RAG, and interactive retrieval. We acknowledged the challenges and open problems that lie ahead, including scalability, adaptability, and evaluation.

As we conclude this exploration, it's clear that RAG is not just a passing trend but a fundamental advancement in the field of natural language processing. It represents a significant step towards building truly intelligent language technologies that can understand, reason, and communicate with us in more meaningful ways.

The journey of RAG is just beginning. As the technology continues to evolve, we can expect to see even more innovative and impactful applications emerge. By embracing the principles of RAG, fostering responsible development, and addressing the challenges ahead, we can unlock its full potential and shape a future where AI is not just intelligent but also ethical, transparent, and beneficial to society.

www.ingramcontent.com/pod-product-compliance
Lightning Source LLC
Chambersburg PA
CBHW080943240526
45469CB00019B/2926